GEEKS WHO CAN SCHMOOZE:

A Credit Suisse Private Banker Tells All

By W. E. Kidd

Copyright Information

This is a work of fiction. All of the characters, organizations, and events portrayed in this novel are either products of the author's imagination or are used fictitiously.

Table of Contents

Dedication

FOR SALLIE MAE

"When I build a fire under a person in it, I do not do it merely because of the enjoyment I get out of seeing him fry, but because he is worth the trouble. It is then a compliment, a distinction; let him give thanks and keep quiet. I do not fry the small, the commonplace, the unworthy." – Mark Twain from his Autobiography.

PART I:

BEFORE THE JOB

CHAPTER ONE

A Bonus Bigger Than Blankfein

On February 18th 2010, *The Wall Street Journal* ran an article with the title, "Credit Suisse Lures Goldman Employees With $11 Million Pay Day." Here's an excerpt from the front page of the "Money and Investing" section:

> "How do you get around all those pay restrictions on Wall Street to collect an eight-digit bonus?
>
> Move to Atlanta.
>
> That is the key takeaway from a heated battle going on between the Atlanta offices of Goldman Sachs Group and Credit Suisse over seven private wealth managers that recently jumped ship from Goldman.
>
> Credit Suisse paid one of the money managers, [Jeremy Jones], $11 million to leave his job at Goldman this month and join CS, according to a lawsuit Goldman filed in federal district court in Atlanta against its former employees. Consider that Jones earned just $1 million for all of last year, according to the lawsuit, and that Goldman's CEO, Lloyd Blankfein, just was awarded $9 million."

In the middle of a major crackdown on Wall Street, Jeremy Jones had just received a bonus bigger than Lloyd Blankfein for doing nothing more than signing a piece of paper. He was also about to sit in an office right in front of my little cubicle. Goldman Sachs was on the sixth floor of our building; we were on the fourth floor, which meant that Jones got up from his desk on the sixth floor, signed some papers, took the elevator down two floors, and sat back down $11 million richer.

Did he bring all of his clients with him? No. How long would it take Credit Suisse to make up that $11 million? A long time. Maybe never. They certainly haven't made it back yet.

During the first week that Jones was at Credit Suisse, I looked over my cubicle wall and saw him sitting in his office. Want to know what $11 million looks like? Everyone else in the office was wearing suits and ties; Jeremy Jones was wearing jeans, a polo and loafers with no socks. That's money. A guy in jeans in an office full of suits.

For Jones, this was brilliant. He was on the winning side of the trade. He had been working at Goldman Sachs since 1997, and those thirteen years before he departed for Credit Suisse had seen a compounded annual growth rate on the S&P 500 of 0.45%. Over his last decade at Goldman Sachs, the S&P 500 had a negative return. His clients may have made money; maybe not. But Jeremy Jones made out like a bandit.

For Credit Suisse and for private banking in general, I have to say that they got caught in a bit of a craze: overpaying for something they deem more valuable than it truly is. It's a craze that I got caught up in, as well. It's why I became a private banker.

Now, here's a little about me. If you are reading this and you want to know what kind of person I am, I'm the guy who read Michael Lewis' *Liar's Poker* and thought it was a how-to guide.

***

Thanks in part to Michael Lewis, my first job out of college was in asset securitization. My senior year I took a fixed income class, which dedicated a portion of the curriculum to collateralized mortgage obligations, and that's when I read *Liar's Poker*. My professor called asset securitization "rocket science finance." Even though Michael Lewis will say that his book was not supposed to encourage people toward following in his footsteps, tell me this blurb from *Liar's Poker* isn't enticing to college kids:

"A chaired professor at the London School of Economics, who took a keen interest in material affairs, stared at me bug-eyed and gurgled when he heard what I was to be paid. It was twice what he earned. He was in his mid-forties and at the top of his profession. I was twenty-four years old and at the bottom of mine. There was no justice in the world, and thank goodness for that."

I was twenty-one when I read that. It was 1998 and afterward all I *wanted* to do was asset securitization. In December of 1998, I got a call from a recruiter at First Union telling me I would receive forty-five thousand dollars per year plus bonus. I was a kid driving my mom's minivan and had huge student loans. Forty-five grand plus bonus. Sold. Thank you, Michael Lewis, for the good advice. In fact, after my first year I would be called into my Managing Director's office and told that my bonus would be thirty-five thousand and that my salary was getting bumped up to sixty-five thousand. At the end of my second year I got a bonus of forty thousand in addition to my sixty-five thousand salary. Twenty-two years-old and making $105,000 in Charlotte, North Carolina, was not too bad in 2000. Do not feel guilty, Mr. Lewis. I loved every second of it. I saved tons of money. I played Liar's Poker every week with bankers and traders.

I never blew anyone up. All of our deals were in heavy equipment (Caterpillar, etc.), and none have defaulted like CMOs and CDOs. I met some of my best friends and I learned some great lessons. I eventually had to leave, but it was mostly because I couldn't see myself doing the job at forty. There were so many other things I wanted to try.

I fell for one of those high-paid finance jobs just like Lewis did. When he wrote about his associate position on Wall Street, he said that there was no justice in the world, and thank goodness for that. Well, I'm here to tell you, there's still no justice in the world. Having joined a Wall Street associate training program after getting my MBA, one fact was abundantly clear: Wall Street will clearly find a way to pay too much for something that it cannot accurately value.

CHAPTER TWO

Where Have All The Stockbrokers Gone?

When was the last time you met someone who said, "I'm a stockbroker." That *is* still a profession, right? Morgan Stanley has about 18,000 of them, but they don't refer to them that way anymore, do they? They are called a financial advisor, planner, investment advisor, wealth manager or private banker.

One of the main reasons that there are no longer any stockbrokers is because they don't make any money. Why pay a guy 2% (the going rate back in the eighties) to process your stock orders when you can just go online to ScottTrade and pay seven bucks a trade? Today, if I go online and create a diverse portfolio of seven ETFs, that costs me a bold fee of $49. Assuming that I spend another $49 rebalancing per quarter, then that's $196 per year. Pretty damn cheap.

If all of Jeremy Jones's clients paid him only $196 per year, then according to the average payout model, he would get to keep about 35% of that revenue for himself. So, to make the one million he apparently made his last year at Goldman Sachs, he would need about 14,577 clients. According to Goldman's complaint, his team of seven only had 140 clients with investment accounts totaling $1.8 billion. He must be doing something more than just processing trades for clients. And, yes, he is doing something more than that. He's giving advice.

Let me break down the entire business for you. Legally, there are only two types of people that can manage investments on the behalf of others: a Registered Investment Advisor and a Registered Representative. The legal title, Registered Representative, is commonly known as a stockbroker. In fact, here's what Wikipedia says about the term:

"A Registered Representative, also called a General Securities Representative, a Stockbroker, or an Account Executive, is an individual who is licensed to sell securities and has the legal power of an agent."

The key takeaway in the description above is "sell securities." Two things happen at the sale of securities. One, a commission is charged. And two, the Rep has a legal obligation to make sure the securities are suitable for the investor. That's all that is involved in being a stockbroker. To enter this business, one must pass a licensing exam called the General Securities Representative Exam or Series 7. This exam takes about six hours.

Now, here's what Wikipedia says about a Registered Investment Advisor:

"The term Registered Investment Advisor (RIA) refers to individuals or firms that receive compensation for giving advice on investing in securities. RIAs are generally paid a percentage of the value of the assets they manage for you."

The RIA is different than a stockbroker because the RIA gets paid to "give advice" and make an annual percentage of your total assets as opposed to just a one-time commission. In exchange for annually collecting a fee that is a percentage of your total assets, the RIA is held to a fiduciary standard. This means that the advisor will act in your best interest for the entire time you do business together. This is a much stronger standard than just making sure an investment is suitable at the time of sale. It also makes it easier to sue an RIA if they give you bad advice. To become an RIA, one must pass the Series 66 in addition to the Series 7. The Series 66 takes two and a half hours. People that invest money for others will use many different titles, but when you boil it down, there are only two options: RIA and Registered Rep.

So, that brings us back to Jeremy Jones. He has passed both his Series 7 and 66! He is an investment advisor. However, he's the fanciest of all investment advisors; a private banker. They are the king of all stockbrokers and investment advisors because they go after the millionaires. These days, it seems like every financial firm has a Private So-and-So's division. All the names are a little different, but using the word "private" seems to be the most important part of the connotation. Note some examples:

Barclays Private Banking. Morgan Stanley Private Wealth Management. Goldman Sachs Private Wealth Management. UBS Private Wealth Management. Bank of America Private Wealth Management. Deutsche Bank Private Wealth Management. Credit Suisse Private Banking. JP Morgan Private Banking. And, JP Morgan Private Wealth Management.

JP Morgan actually has two private divisions! Yeah, that's not confusing. It's like Jamie Dimon, CEO of JP Morgan, looked at Goldman Sachs' title of Private Wealth Management, but also saw that Credit Suisse had Private Banking and liked the sound of that, too. I can imagine the meeting to decide the names of the groups and how that went:

"Dear Board of Directors, in an effort to confuse our employees and mess with our competitors, I have come to a decision on the matter concerning the titles Private Wealth Management and Private Banking. Fuck it. Let's use both!"

What's so private, anyway? That's what I want to know. If your account is held anywhere in the United States, with any bank or financial company, domestic or not, that company reports all of your information to the United States government. That's not private at all. If by "private" the firms mean that they don't put your statements on the Internet on a site that allows your neighbor to see your bank account, then yes, they are private. So is every other bank account in the country.

Then what exactly *is* so private? Your account information isn't private; it is automatically reported to the IRS. On the other hand, if you have an account in Switzerland, this information is not reported to the IRS by the bank. It is the account holder's responsibility to report that information to the government. So in a sense, this type of account is private. It also pisses off tax collectors and is why Obama is trying to crack down on Swiss banking privacy. However, I'm not talking about off-shore accounts. I'm talking about accounts held in the United States.

In short, "private" is no longer a description of the client's information; it's a description of the bankers themselves. Much like a fancy golf course asserting, "This is a private course," banks now do a similar thing. Private banking is a private course. "If you can't meet our million-dollar minimums, then you don't have access to our exclusive private bankers only reserved for millionaires."

That's some clever marketing, huh? What used to refer to client privacy has now been turned into a term to describe the banker's exclusivity. The name is all about the banker and not the client. If someone wants a private account, it doesn't exist legally in the United States.

If you want to be truly accurate about where the term private banking comes from, it originally referred to the opposite of the public sector banks, known as Stadtwechsel (city exchequers), which grew out of the public exchange offices in the late Middle Ages. Yes, my fellow Americans, I said the middle ages. These public sector banks lost ground to the private banks in the 18th century. During that time, the ruling houses that controlled all sectors of the European economy found that they needed a great deal more capital. Thus, investment activity in Europe was in demand, creating perfect economic conditions for the rise of private banking institutions. "Private" meaning that it was not owned by the government.

So, if you want to use the term the way it was originally conceived, a private bank is one that is not held by the government. In this case, Northeast Georgia Bank is a private bank. But does Northeast Georgia Bank have private banking? No.

CHAPTER THREE

The Interview

During my entire four year career at First Union/Wachovia/Wells Fargo/whatever you want to call it, I didn't have one person from my Alma Mater contact me for advice on how to get a job at the firm. I was the guy undergraduates would have to interview with on their Super Saturday (which is the final round of interviews for undergraduate students wanting to become investment bankers), yet no one ever emailed me or called me ahead of time to ask how I got my job and whether I liked it. I also worked at Merrill Lynch and Bear Stearns in the late 90's, and no one ever asked me how to get a job or passed a resume to me there, either.

By contrast, during my first twelve months at Credit Suisse in private banking, I had seventeen people reach out to me with their resume. That's right, more than one per month. I'm a nice guy and I helped everyone–a few even got offers in Credit Suisse Atlanta, Philadelphia and Singapore offices. What I want you to know about that, though, is that there are two ways to get this job: by the rules and by breaking the rules. I prefer breaking the rules – that's how I got my job.

Here's how I did it and how easy it was and the questions that were asked. In October of the first year of my MBA program, all the finance students took a trek to New York to meet with all the firms on the Street, and got hosted by Human Resources people for jobs in investment banking. The week was capped off with a party on the floor of the New York Stock Exchange at night. (Duncan Niederauer, the CEO of the New York Stock Exchange, received his MBA from Emory and I think he gives the school a good deal on renting out the NYSE floor.) This event had been becoming a bit of a tradition, so we went around to all the big banks in October

2007 just before everything was wiped out. We went to Lehman, Bear Sterns, and Merrill Lynch: all the big blow-ups. Plus, we went to the survivors: Credit Suisse, UBS, Goldman Sachs, JP Morgan, and Citi.

At the end of these investment banking informational events, all the students would swarm the investment banking recruiters, but I would hang back, drink their free drinks, wait for the swarm to end, and then ask for the name of the private banking recruiter. Typically, the investment banking recruiter would say, "Send me your resume and I'll get it to the private banking recruiter." I did this at every bank we visited and Credit Suisse moved the fastest. The week after I got back from the New York trek, the head of Atlanta's Credit Suisse office called me and said, "Why don't you come over to the office next week and spend the day with us."

I accepted his offer and thought we were just going to have an informational interview where I got to ask a few questions and find out about the job and the bank. When I arrived at the Credit Suisse office, it had a country club feel to it. It was very clean and quiet, with wood paneling and some faux gold at the entrance to the suite. My first meeting was with the head of the office, Michael Sterling. Sterling came into money by marrying the daughter of the guy who founded Aaron's Rent-A-Center, Charlie Loudermilk. Sterling lives in a mansion next to the Governor's house. Sterling is a nice guy, but he got fired from Credit Suisse during my second year in MBA. We'll get into that later.

That day, Sterling said that he wanted me to meet with two people: Jeremy Smith and Rob Weaver. Smith looks and talks like Alan Alda and he was the easiest interview of all time. His questions were basically, "Tell me about yourself." "Why do you want to do this job?" "What gives you satisfaction in the job?" Then, the rest of the interview was us chatting about Louisville because we had both lived there, and me asking him the standard questions about himself. "When did you start working at Credit Suisse?" "What do you think about the market right now?" "How do you manage assets for your clients?" I think he spoke more in the interview than I did.

After our brief meeting, Smith left and Rob Weaver entered the room to interview me. Weaver said that he only had about fifteen minutes because he had a tee time at Peachtree Golf Club and had to leave. That was the first time I realized how little work actually is done in private banking. Playing golf at ten a.m. on a weekday is normal business. Being in the office is not important. Rob actually came through with some good finance questions after the obligatory "Walk me through your resume." He asked me to pitch him a stock and he asked, "What's the yield curve?" Not a bad question and slightly more challenging than Smith.

I pitched Weaver Google and explained that the yield curve is the spread between treasuries and Libor. It is typically inverted before a recession and was inverted at the beginning of that year. That was it. End of interview.

I walked back to Sterling's office and we chatted for a bit about high school football because my cousin was the starting quarterback at his high school alma mater. His only question was for me to define success. I said something to the effect of no debt and a beautiful wife who knows how to cook. Really cook. Not just can-of-mushroom-soup-plus-other-stuff cook. Sterling married into millions and I always wondered what he thought about my answer. It must have been something like, "Wow, low standards. I thought he would have said golf membership at Augusta National." Or, maybe he thought to himself "Wow, W.E. Kidd has figured out the secret to life." He probably went with the former.

Two weeks after my interview at Credit Suisse, Sterling called me and said that he was giving me an offer for a summer internship. The associate's salary was $95,000 per year (now it's $100,000) and I would be getting the equivalent of that paycheck every two weeks over the ten-week summer. This is roughly $18,000 plus a $2,000 moving bonus, which I would get even if I didn't need to move. It was November 2007 and I had been in my

MBA program for about three months and already had an offer for the job that I would have through 2011. I was the first person in my class to get an offer. Did I accept it right away? No, of course not.

There's something inherently stupid about MBA programs that makes you think you have to shop around offers. So, that's exactly what I did: I went to Goldman Sachs and sat down in a conference room with Craig Smiley, the head of training for their private wealth management department, and told him about my offer. I was a cocky bastard and he said that Goldman had a formal process that entails an interview on campus in February and then Super Saturday after that.

I walked out of that Goldman Sachs office and called Sterling on his cell, and told him I would accept his offer at Credit Suisse. As it turned out, Smiley would do just about the same thing two years later, and sit right in front of me and next to Jeremy Jones. He was one of the seven bankers who *The Wall Street Journal* described as coming over to Credit Suisse with Jeremy Jones.

I have said that there's a "by the rules" way to get a job in private banking and a rule-breaking way. What Craig Smiley described with all that formal interview process and Super Saturday jargon was rule following, which typically went something like this: you would submit your resume on campus in December and then Goldman would select a few of those resumes to interview on campus in February. Then, they would ask the on-campus interviewees to come to the office for a Super Saturday round of interviews, which is usually around eight interviews in one day. Then, you get the offer, or not. There would also be a lot of coffees and conference calls with current employees in between all the interviewing. You would then typically get your offer in March.

You can see why my "not by the rules" way was a little better. I interviewed once and got an offer four months before everyone else. Even though Craig Smiley, head of all training at Goldman

Sachs, wouldn't break the rules for me, I find it very funny that he followed in my footsteps over to Credit Suisse.

Before moving along, I will describe one more way to get into a private banking associate program. I think this might be the best of all. As stated earlier, I got seventeen resumes during my first year at Credit Suisse and helped a few job seekers get offers. One of those people was an Emory undergrad who had spent a few years in pharmaceutical sales. He asked if I could help him get in the door. Since I like doing things not by the books, I was intrigued. This guy didn't even have his MBA, but I pushed his resume to the top of the pile, got him the interviews, coached him on exactly what was going to be said and interviewers' personalities and he nailed it! He got the job without an MBA. And, I got a $3,000 new hire bonus for finding him. Win-win.

The point here is that there are no technical finance questions asked in these interviews. From what I've seen, if you actually want the job you can get it without knowing anything whatsoever about finance. And, getting the job before getting an MBA is genius because now when this guy has no clients in twelve months, he can start applying for an MBA instead of looking for a new job because he's basically done no real work and has no finance experience.

CHAPTER FOUR

Wall Street **The Movie 1987 vs. 2010**

I'm assuming that everyone reading this has seen the movie *Wall Street*. Bud Fox. Greed Is Good. Blue Horseshoe loves Anacott Steel. It's a classic. It's also proof that stockbrokers don't exist anymore. If you read any summary of the movie, it generally starts out with, "Stockbroker Bud Fox....etc." Even in the February 19, 2011 *Wall Street Journal*, under the title *Wall Street* and a picture of Bud Fox, there is a blurb that begins, "Ambitions stockbroker Bud Fox..." There is no doubt in anyone's mind that Bud Fox was a stockbroker. He sat at his desk with a phonebook in front of him, called people out of that phonebook and pitched stocks.

Remember what a big fucking deal it was when Bud was calling on Gekko? His little reminder came up in Matrix dos prompt grey telling him to call Gekko on his birthday. And, John C. McGinley says something to the effect of, "Whoa...calling the whale today." I should stop for a second and tell you that John C. McGinley's brother is a private banker at Credit Suisse and looks and talks like John. It's probably half the reason why he has so many clients, but back to the movie. Bud Fox called a millionaire and it was a huge fucking deal. John C. McGinley looked at Bud as if to say, "no way in hell are you getting that guy as a client." I made that call about a hundred times a week because that's what being a private banking associate is. It's that scene over and over.

Bud Fox was a stockbroker. In 1987, stockbrokers existed. Stockbrokers were what everyone thought of when they thought of Wall Street. So, Oliver Stone made a movie and made the lead character a stockbroker. His father was a stockbroker and everyone knows that you write what you know. Flash forward to 2010. If Oliver Stone made a movie about a stockbroker calling people and pitching stocks over the phone, people would laugh. It just doesn't happen anymore. By today's standards, the whole concept of the movie is ridiculous. Your stockbroker becomes your M&A originator and president of a publicly traded airline? It's a little far-fetched.

However, Bud Fox is a great example of what became of private banking. Now, let's say that Bud and Gekko didn't partake in any illegal activity and they actually just invested in stocks and had a legal broker/client relationship. Their first trade together was 20,000 shares of Blue Star at 15.16. That's $303,200. Bud jumps out of his chair at the opportunity and says, "I bagged the elephant." And, John C. McGinley makes the greatest "no fucking way" face and ominously says "Gecko…"

It's great fun, but my boss would be pretty pissed off at me for that and would advise me to not take the assets unless we can get some more from the client. He would want about 2 – 3 million or nothing. The difference being, Bud made good money on that trade in the 80's. In the 80's he got 1-2% or $3,000-6,000 and today would only get $7. After the Blue Star trade went well, Gordon gave Bud $1 million. Back in the 80's, $1 million meant something.

Now assume there was no illegal stuff in the movie. We flash forward to today and Gekko hit the $50 million number that he describes as his dream number of being wealthy. And, let's assume that Bud is his only broker and the seven that Gordon referenced in his first scene in *Wall Street* all got fired. Bud would no longer be a stockbroker would he? He would be a private banker. Burnham Steinham would have created a private banking division and Bud would be in it. Sure he could still place trades for Gekko, but he'd probably want to move to a wrap fee instead of transaction-based business. And, he would no longer be pitching stocks that he researched on his own. He would have economists, investment officers, and managers all giving him information on stocks, bonds, private equity, hedge funds, trust and estate planning, tax planning, and structured notes.

If Gekko never went to jail, then in the second movie he would probably be more interested in tax planning than running a hedge fund. The movie would have some sweet name like *Wall Street II: The Death Tax Never Sleeps.* The whole movie in my mind would be about Gekko efficiently passing assets to his daughter and keeping Shia LaBouef out of his estate plans because LaBouef sucks and ruins all things good that came out of the 80's. I would probably go see that. "LaBouef...you'll get nothing and like it!" That line would be in the trailer.

CHAPTER FIVE

Summer Internship

A job as a summer associate at a big name firm is very important when getting your MBA. If you can imagine the very rich talking about where they are "summering," it is similar to that. Going to a good Wall Street firm is like going to the Hamptons or the south of France. It's where you want to be. Going to a firm or getting a summer internship that no one has ever heard of is like saying you are going to Port Orange, Florida, for the summer. At least there is water and sun, you say to yourself. By the end of your first year of MBA that's all anyone talks about. *Where are you summering? What are you doing for the summer?* If you don't have a good answer, your life sucks. Ten weeks later the only question will be, "Did you get an offer?"

I was happy with my choice of Credit Suisse. First, it didn't disappear like Bear Stearns, Lehman Brothers or Merrill Lynch. Second, it kept its name out of the papers. And third, it would be the largest Swiss bank by market cap at the end of the financial crisis. It never took money from any government. It never got sued by the United States government. Plus, private banking might just be its strongest point as opposed to sales and trading or investment banking. All of these factors were important because the whole point of a summer associate position is to get an offer at the end of the summer. You needed your firm to be around at the end of summer to get an offer. In the summer of 2008, this was not a sure thing.

I'm going to take the summer associate program as an opportunity to introduce a character. When I say "character", I mean someone who is represented in my story, but also the other meaning of odd or unusual. The internship began with all the

MBAs from around the country spending the first week in New York before going back to regional offices (my office was in Atlanta). There was another summer associate who would be in the Atlanta office, and this is "the character."

It was the first day of our high-powered new jobs in New York and everyone arrived wearing dark colored suits— except one guy. He arrived wearing a wrinkled tan suit with some old brown shoes and a brown belt. He was a total schlepper. I think every employee across the globe, all 52,000, were wearing dark suits that day. If there was a fire drill at Credit Suisse and the entire bank had evacuated Eleven Madison, you could have seen this guy from outer space. One tan suit dot standing in Madison Square Park, surrounded by thousands of dark suit dots. He looked ridiculous and I remember hearing someone whisper the name, "Matlock." He was from Atlanta and wore cheap suits. It was the perfect nickname.

Starting my summer at Credit Suisse's New York office was fantastic. I could grab a milkshake at the Shake Shack or cocktails at 11 Madison Park. I was seconds away from iconic New York summer fun. During that first week, I did all the typical Wall Street training. Sat in a dark room and did capital markets review and accounting. Took a trip to the Bloomberg building and ate their free snacks in their high tech building. Sat and listened to the heads of groups from around the bank tell me about the firm's greatness. It was really more about them selling *me* at that point and they did a good job with it. At the end of that first week all ten summer associates flew back to our regional offices and then it was our turn to sell.

Arriving in the Atlanta office that summer, I realized just how bad the market had become and how bad the job market was going to be if I didn't get an offer at the end of the summer. All the private bankers in the office were in a bad mood. The stock market was getting crushed. Some private bankers had clients in risky investments that were down 70%. Some had clients in asset-backed commercial paper. There was very little to be happy about. When I would ask private bankers about the hardest part of their job, everyone said that losing money for a client was the toughest part. That was a universal answer all that summer. The whole vibe of the office was awful and very quiet; I had to look past that fact and sell myself.

A piece of selling I had to do was to get on a conference call with all the other associates and the head of training, Eric Dale, every Friday to pitch an investable idea I developed from listening to the morning research calls. For instance, the price of oil had hit $120 that summer and Credit Suisse's economists believed it had peaked. So, that same week the bank came out with a structured note that would make money if the price of oil went down. I would get on the call and talk about the price of oil, what I learned from the internal economists that week, and then tie it all in with the oil investment offering. In fact, the oil structured note was quite popular to pitch the week it came out.

Eric Dale, who would critique us every week, is from Scotland and is an old weathered private banker. He is the type who could expound on quite possibly anything, was known for his ability to get off subject and ramble about his escapades of days long ago getting Middle Eastern Royalty to open accounts, and loved to tell the same stories over and over. He also loved repeating the same sayings in his thick Scottish accent. "W.E., sometimes the light at the end of the tunnel could be a train." "W.E., if hard work were king, the donkey would be the king of the jungle." These were among his favorites.

Eric was always supportive except when we would have to get on these calls. Then, the evil Eric would come out. There was very little hazing in our program, but this was basically a way for you to get hazed and see if you could respond professionally. If your ideas weren't laid out in a coherent fashion, you would get destroyed and everyone would hear it. If you couldn't answer some tough questions about your idea, Eric would do his best to embarrass you.

Matlock and I would actually do an okay job of holding our own, but there was a guy from Boston who just didn't get it. He would never use research to support his ideas and couldn't answer any question that Eric shot at him. Week after week we would wait to hear if Boston would wise up, but week after week he would not bring anything to the call. In front of everyone, Eric would let him have it. "Frankly, I don't care what you have to say or what your opinions are. What is the bank's opinion?" "That is the most illogical nonsense we've heard all summer." "You better actually put some thought into this next week." "What have you been doing all week? Not listening to the research call I suppose. Are they too early in the morning for you? You should wake up earlier." Boston guy was doomed.

Another sale I would have to do was to the private bankers in the office. Each week Matlock and I would have to rotate around and work for different bankers. The office is broken into six teams of two to three private bankers. The team concept basically came about during the nineties when the "broker" began to die out and the "private banker" and "wealth manager" started to rise. Brokers began teaming up. Maybe one would have a focus on covering pension funds and the other would have a focus on family offices and they would team up to get more business together. The sale was that now instead of having one guy pitching you stocks, you had a team covering your financial needs. The brokers would split the revenue they brought in and since there were two of them with different types of clients, their paychecks would be a little more stable.

Matlock and I rotated around, working for different people in the office, and it was an awful time to try and convince someone you wanted to be a private banker. No one was bringing in new accounts and the assets they had under management were going down. There I was saying that I wanted to come into their office and compete with them to open new accounts in the worst market any private banker had ever seen. Competing is truly what I would be doing. When someone in Atlanta sells a business and takes in a bunch of money, both the experienced private banker and I will want to get this guy as a client and only one will be able to win. The more private bankers in the office, the more competition.

The rotations didn't really have anything to do with finance – just about getting people to like me. Matlock, within five minutes of meeting someone, would tell them where he went to high school and that his "daydee ees ah lawyeeer." When you don't go to a top college or grad school, I suppose you tell people where you went to high school. There wasn't one day that he didn't talk about his high school or his dad and it drove me crazy. There wasn't one day that he got in before me or left after me. And, there wasn't one thing he did all summer that involved math or finance. In fact, he would often say that "numbers aren't my strong point."

I would do my best to get private bankers to give me projects that would show I had a brain and was passionate about finance. I would put in more hours. Matlock would get in late, leave early and talk about his high school and *daayd*. Those were basically our strategies when rotating around on teams and getting to know people in the office. The ultimate goal was for the private bankers to tell the office manager that I was good guy.

The biggest sale I would have to make would be at the end of the summer. The last week of the internship, all the MBA interns from around the country would fly back to New York to give a presentation on an investment that Credit Suisse was offering clients. Most people would pitch hedge funds or private equity. I chose to focus on an investment that the firm was offering to clients to harness the volatility of the market using call and put spreads. It was complex, but there was a lot of volatility in the market at the time and I thought it was a compelling investment.

The last week of summer, after schmoozing all the brokers in the office, and intelligently presenting ideas on the weekly call, I flew back to New York to pitch my investment to senior management in the private bank. All ten summer associates reunited for our final hurdle in our ten-week interview. I had my slides. I had my spiel down. I thought it was smart. It flowed. It showed off my knowledge of options. And, it was timely because it performed well in volatile markets – exactly what we were experiencing.

All of us jammed ourselves into a conference room in the underground levels of Eleven Madison and did our best to impress. I paced back and forth outside the room and tried not to think about what would happen if I failed or came up short. There was so much at stake. I needed to return to school with a guaranteed job, which was going to be difficult in the middle of the worst recession since the 1930's. I was going to have about $130k in student loans when I graduated. I needed a good job. I had been getting in first and leaving last all summer. I'd held my own on our conference calls and schmoozed everyone in the office. All I had to do was go into that room and give an intelligent presentation. I paced back and forth, went over my presentation in my head before I walked into the conference room. Nervous and confident.

I addressed the room and introduced the investment I would be presenting. I used stories and addressed attendees by name in my examples. I covered the math behind the investment and used simple graphs to drive my point home. I flowed through the beginning middle and end. And, I tried to avoid making eye contact with the other summer interns staring at me – they just made me nervous. I was "on" for ten minutes and then held Q&A. I did a decent job answering and deflecting questions. Then, I sat down as the next person got up to present. All of that work all summer for ten minutes. I was done and had an empty feeling in my stomach. There was nothing left to do to get the job. It was out of my hands.

I won't dwell too much on other's presentations except to say that Matlock blew it. This was the first time during our summer that he would actually have to present his work to people and he sounded ridiculous. He didn't really understand the investment and the audience pounced. He was interrupted very quickly during his presentation and grilled because no one understood what he was talking about. The person that interrupted apologized and then let him finish before grilling him some more. One of the many things wrong with his presentation was that he was pitching an idea that had a negative return and was underperforming the S&P 500.

"This has a negative return. Why did you even pick this?" One of the graders asked. Matlock was flustered beyond belief. It was tough to watch. In New York, no one knew his dad or his high school. Leaving him to his own ideas and presentation skills was poignantly sad and pathetic. Even his attitude projected that he felt it unfair that he had to endure the humiliation of presenting his own thoughts.

I flew back to Atlanta and got my feedback in an email, and was told that I was "witty with good structure and poise." My negative input was that I "seemed a little nervous." I agreed with both positive and negative. Matlock would not say what his feedback was.

The office manager, Michael Sterling, called both of us into his office and told us what his thoughts were of the two of us.

"W.E., you are the brains," he said. "And, Matlock, you are more of a social person."

In my mind this was the ultimate compliment. They recognized that I was the smarter one. At least there was that. It was our last day and we were told that we would get a call during the week whether we were getting an offer or not. That was it. My summer associate job was over. I waited three days…I got the call…the offer:

"$60k signing bonus…$95k salary plus year-end bonus…You'll begin training with a month in Zurich, Switzerland, then we'll fly you to New York for another month…Of course your wife can visit."

I accepted in a second because it was 2008 and I had just gotten a great job while the rest of the world was falling apart. I could pay my student loans and could look forward to life not sucking.

Seven of the ten summer associates would get offers. Matlock would be one of them. It made sense. He was just like the office manager, who didn't know much about finance, but had a good family. I had to overcome my lack of family with my brain. Thank God it worked. People around the country were losing their jobs, their homes and their retirement money, but I had just been given an amazing job at the biggest Swiss bank in the world.

My dad was one of those unlucky ones who lost his job—he was forced into early retirement. I felt half-guilty for landing a great job on one hand, and half-guilty on the other for *needing* that great job. Without it, I was dead: laden with a massive amount of student loans. I could never make ends meet without the big signing bonus and salary I was being offered.

Sallie Mae guessed right when it made *me* a loan. The credit officer must have seen earning potential and determination in my application. Once you've sold a piece of your soul to Sallie Mae, why not sell the rest to Wall Street?

CHAPTER SIX

I Want To Be A Stockbroker

I always wanted to be a stockbroker. When I was in kindergarten in Chicago in the early eighties, for parent's day at my school, the teacher created a wall with everyone's name on it that listed what we wanted to be when we grew up. Most everyone said doctor, lawyer, football player, astronaut, that kind of thing. I was only five years old and racked my brain to think of the word "stockbroker." I had no idea what exactly a stockbroker did when I was five, but I had heard adults use the word and I liked the sound of it.

When it was my turn to tell the teacher what I wanted to be, I said, "I can't remember the name for it, but it's a guy in a suit who makes money."

She listed off a couple things. "Lawyer?"

"No."

"Businessman?"

"No."

"Stockbroker?"

"Yes!"

When my parents came to school and saw, "W.E. Kidd– Stockbroker," they thought it was very strange. I was definitely the only kid with "stockbroker" listed next to their name. My parents asked me why I wanted to be a stockbroker. Who knew that people from Goldman Sachs, Credit Suisse and JP Morgan would be asking me that same question twenty-five years later? It would have been great if little five-year old me would have said, "I want more client interaction," like all private banking interviewees say. I told my parents that I'd heard my dad's friend Mike talk about the job. I really liked Mike because he drove a Pontiac Firebird. Mike would also be the person to rent *Wall Street* for me on Beta when it first came out in 1987. I was ten years-old and he rented me an R-rated movie. Add in the whole Firebird thing and Mike was cool.

Over the years I would play finance video games as a kid. "Wall Street Kid" video game on Nintendo in 1990 was a godsend for me. I didn't stop playing until I won the whole thing. The same goes for the PC game, "Rags to Riches: The Financial Market Simulation Game." I was obsessed with money and the stock market. I would eventually read my first finance book, Peter Lynch's *Learn to Earn* in 1996. I opened my first E-Trade Account that same year. I would go on to major in Finance at Emory University and have my first finance internship ever at Bear Stearns in their private client services group for a broker named Charlie Barry from 1997 - 1998.

During every single one of my summer associate interviews, I would say that the reason I wanted to be a private banker was because of Charlie Barry. Charlie Barry, in my mind, was the quintessential stockbroker. He might have been the last stockbroker in existence. Charlie was a fast talking broker from New York. He had gone to New York City College and started at Merrill Lynch in the early eighties before making his way over to Lehman Brothers in 1984. He eventually started working out of the Lehman Brothers office in Atlanta in the nineties and then in the Atlanta Bear Stearns office by the time that I met up with him.

Charlie had posted an internship offering at Emory and I jumped at the opportunity. I drove my mom's minivan to meet with him and wore the one shabby suit that I owned. I got the internship, which was for twenty hours a week paid. I would continue to drive my mom's minivan to Bear Stearns and wear the same shabby suit every time. In Charlie's office I would have a desk next to his with a computer I would use to do research for him, make prospect lists, and submit trades to the cage. I was told by someone in the office that if I kept my mouth shut and my ears open I would be a good intern. So, that's what I did. In doing so, I picked up on a lot of Charlie's spiel and how he pitched.

The one thing he loved the most to do to his clients was to call them up and if he got an assistant he would say, "Tell him it's his wife's divorce attorney."

That line was absolutely classic Charlie. In 1997 he was insanely bullish on Qualcomm. He had everyone in Qualcomm.

"You're either in Qualcomm or you're not my client. I've got my kid's college fund in Qualcomm," he would say.

You couldn't walk into his office and not hear him say "Qualcomm" or "Qualycomm" as he liked to call it sometimes. He also loved Pfizer–they'd just come out with Viagra. "This stock is going straight up!" he would say.

He spoke a mile a minute, had a great New York accent, and was on the phone from the time the market opened to about a half an hour after it closed. He was one of my best bosses. He paid me more than he should have and treated me like I was important even though I wasn't. I would think about Charlie Barry a lot over the years especially because Qualcomm was the best performing stock in 1999. It surged twenty-six hundred percent! I imagined that Charlie had at least $100,000 of his own personal money in Qualcomm and that it had turned into $2.6 million in one year. I imagined him crushing it and retiring. He was already doing well and living in Chipper Jones' neighborhood in 1997.

I lost track of Charlie and years later I called Bear Stearns. Charlie wasn't there any longer and no one could tell me where he went or give me any information. I couldn't find anything on the Internet either. I just imagined him as a millionaire on a beach. In 2007, when I was in my first year of my MBA, I would say, " Okay, I'm ready to be like Charlie Barry now. I've matured enough to do the job."

CHAPTER SEVEN

My First Day

My first day at Credit Suisse was a dream come true. When I was an undergrad in the nineties, my grandmother bought me a book called *The Numbered Account* by Christopher Reich. My grandmother was a great big Italian woman who lived to please her grandchildren. She was a strong-willed Calabrese who was always on the hunt for books to give me. Like all grandmothers, when you tell them what to buy you, it always turns out well, but when they branch out on their own, it usually turns into disaster.

My grandmother knew I liked books, so that was what I always got from her. Books, books, books. She was always trying to surprise me with new authors, but her surprises never worked except for one time. I had never asked for *The Numbered Account* or even heard of it. Maybe she was thinking that it was like a finance version of *The Firm*, which I really loved when I was in high school. The more likely scenario was she just got lucky. She would probably box my ears for writing that.

The beginning of *The Numbered Account* paints the picture of a newly minted MBA flying to Switzerland to start his new job as a Swiss banker; he has a beautiful fiancée, the Swiss landscapes are amazing, and I loved Reich's description of Banhofstrasse, the street where Credit Suisse has its headquarters. At the time I read it, I never would have thought I would get to have a similar experience, but that's the type of adventure I was about to embark upon.

I had just graduated from MBA, I kissed my beautiful newlywed wife at the airport and caught a plane to Zurich for dinner with my associate class. I packed four books with me for the trip: *Series 7 License Exam Manuel, Series 66 License Exam Manuel, Fodor's Switzerland,* and *From Those Wonderful Folks*

Who Gave You Pearl Harbor by Jerry Della Famina. Della Famina is one of the great American salesmen and I thought I could learn something from him. I flipped between all of my books during the flight and when the plane landed, I was officially a Swiss banker in Switzerland.

After arriving, I was extremely jet-lagged, but wouldn't miss my first job assignment, which was to eat dinner with my fellow associates from around the globe. I took a cab to my hotel and thought my room was very big and what I would call Swiss modern. It reminded me of The Standard or something like that. When I entered my hotel room, there was a facebook of all the new associates from around the world – twenty-six in total. There was a schedule for our month in Zurich, a tram pass, and a map of Zurich. These materials combined with my finance books and guide to Zurich restaurants was all I really needed for the rest of the month. I put on a suit and went to dinner to meet the rest of the class.

I got there just before everyone was to sit down for the official welcome. I grabbed a glass of wine and found a seat. It was all very impressive. Grand ballroom. White table cloths. Everyone in their suits. There were some opening remarks from the woman who ran the training program and then we were to each stand up and introduce ourselves: name, school, and city we would be working in.

I was impressed and intimidated. Almost everyone had to be smarter than me.

One Oxford graduate - Dubai. Two University of Chicago graduates - Geneva and Chicago. Two Northwestern graduates - Chicago. Three NYU graduates - Madrid and New York. One University of Virginia graduate - New York. One Dartmouth graduate - New York. Three INSEAD graduates - Zurich. Four London Business School graduates - Zurich, Geneva and London. One HEC graduate - Zurich. One City University London graduate - London. One Brigham Young graduate - San Francisco. One

SMU graduate - Dallas. One UGA graduate - Atlanta. And, then
there was me – Emory University working in the Atlanta office. As
I stood up and said my name, my school and the office I would
work out of, I thought everyone was looking at me and thinking of
the Atlanta quote from *Liar's Poker*:

"Selling municipal bonds in Atlanta was unthinkably wretched.
Trading mortgages in New York was mouthwateringly good."

Managing money for millionaires out of the Atlanta office
would definitely involve selling municipal bonds. "Great," I
thought to myself, "everyone here thinks I'm wretched."

The first friend I made was the HEC graduate; he and I sat next
to each other at dinner and I discovered he had already been
working in Zurich for a few months. Apparently he had a kick-ass
apartment and knew his way around the city. He *looked* like a
private banker–Gucci everything down to a flashy Gucci belt. He
dressed the part.

The first day of work was good. Everyone was a blank sheet at
that point. No personalities, just résumés in suits. At that first
dinner a tone had already been set: look good and work hard. The
way you present yourself is very important. I took notice of these
things, knocked back a few glasses of wine and passed when folks
asked if I wanted to go out on the town. Not that night. It was
about three a.m. EST and I had about four glasses of wine. I
walked back to my room, Skyped my wife and went to sleep with
dreams of Swiss banking riches in my head.

Chapter Eight

Paradeplatz 8

The short story "Rich Boy" by F. Scott Fitzgerald begins with this passage:

> "Let me tell you about the very rich. They are different from you and me. They possess and enjoy early, and it does something to them, makes them soft where we are hard and cynical where we are trustful, in a way that unless you were born rich, it is very difficult to understand. They think deep in their hearts that they are better than we are because we had to discover the compensations and refuges of life ourselves. Even when they enter deep into our world or sink below us, they still think that they are better than we are. They are different."

Those first few days of training were about possessing and enjoying early. Each day went on in much the same fashion. The bank would haul in a bunch of important people from every possible department and then we would go on an expensive lunch, a tour, and share a ridiculously expensive dinner.

When I first arrived in my hotel room I was given a schedule for the first three days. Day one would have us lunching at Juan Costa, touring Credit Suisse headquarters, and dining at Zunfthaus zug Waag, one of the oldest guild houses in Zurich. What immediately jumped off the page at me was the tour of Credit Suisse headquarters. It impressed upon me secret gold chambers, hidden treasures from long ago and spy games.

Day two was lunch at Enigmatt, a walking Zurich City tour, and dinner at Belvoirpark hosted by Christian Machate, the head of Human Resources for Credit Suisse for the world.

Our third and final day of possessing and enjoying early would include a meeting with Walter Berchtold, the head of private banking for the entire firm, lunch at Bederstrasse and dinner at a restaurant in the hills overlooking Lake Zurich. In between the lunches and tours, people from around the bank would tell us about their department and the bank's history and culture. Everyone had great Swiss Banking names like Lars, Luzi, Bastian, and my favorite Jan vonder Muhll.

The training took place on Bederstrasse, a couple blocks from the hotel and a few tram stops from Credit Suisse headquarters on Paradeplatz. I walked to the Credit Suisse building that first morning with a sense of purpose and accomplishment. I had made it. I was destined to do this. Wearing my new suit and carrying my new briefcase that my wife bought me for graduation, I made my way down Bederstrasse on a nice, crisp Zurich summer morning.

My first introduction to Credit Suisse and Swiss banking history was from Johannes Hennekeuser, Head of Production Support. Johannes was a typical Zurich Swiss bank employee. Thin. Dark, well-fitting suit. Short cropped hair. Dark rimmed hipster glasses. That is a Zurich banker. He was a nice guy. He was a polished presenter and painted a picture of the firm where I would be starting my career. Some might have called him boring, but he was the first guy I had heard, so I wasn't quick to judge yet. Three days of speeches and the spiel would get a little tedious, but I truly loved every second of it.

Our first excursion out of the classroom was what I had been waiting for: a tour of Credit Suisse headquarters. All of us hopped on a tram, dressed in our best suits, which actually fit in quite well, and traveled a few stops to the private banking capital of the world – Paradeplatz, which literally translates to Parade Square. It is on

Bahnhofstrasse, known as the most expensive street in the world because of its luxury shopping.

Credit Suisse headquarters is located on Bahnhofstrasse at Paradeplatz. Swiss banking rival UBS is about one hundred feet away, just across the street. At one time there was a treasure trove hidden under Bahnhofstrasse. Piles upon piles of gold were once hidden in subterranean vaults beneath the street. Word has it that all the gold has been moved away from the banks to a site near the airport. Getting off the tram at Paradeplatz was amazing. The thoughts that ran through my head ranged from Jason Bourne and secret vaults, to pride for getting to walk into the biggest Swiss bank in the world as an employee.

Paradeplatz 8 is a beautiful building built in 1876 by the Pfister brothers. Not only is it part of the Swiss national image, it is a hallmark of the financial world. Credit Suisse actually has several significant buildings ranging from a 300-year old baroque manor called Bocken in Horgen that is known for its impressive wine cellar, to a branch in Chiasso Italy built in 1993 by architects Sergio Grassi and Sendro Centoni, which is ultra-modern.

The main office on Paradeplatz is a combination of the old and the new. The decorative façade is undoubtedly 1876 baroque with ornate stone carved figurines, balconies and pediments. It makes the UBS building across the street look stark and naked. I'm sure some would say Credit Suisse looks like a pretentious wedding cake. Also, to picture it in your mind's eye, both are only about five stories tall and a few blocks from the lake: there are no skyscrapers in Zurich.

When approaching the entrance to the headquarters, I was sucked into the Lichtohof. No, the Lichtohof is not a monster or dragon keeping robbers away from the gold, but rather is German for "The Atrium." The atrium is modern: renovated by the firm Atelier 5 in 2002. At its center there is a waterless fountain designed by the artist Silvie Defraoui. The waterless fountain is filled with neon light and scrolling digital wishes that money cannot buy. For instance, the word "love" might flash past. Above the fountain are massive skylights and three passages converge at the fountain: one from Paradeplatz, one from Bahnhofstrasse, and one from Barengasse. The passages are filled with shops: Armani, Zegna, Cartier, Montblanc, and of course the entrance to Credit Suisse where it has been since 1876. All in all, a clean sleek arcade and atrium.

To enter the Credit Suisse building I had to go through a set of Bourne Identity-esque doors. There were two sets of sliding glass doors. The first set of doors opened, I walked in, the doors closed behind me and I was essentially in a small glass room for a few seconds. Then, the second set of doors opened in front of me and I walked through.

Each associate in our class did this one at a time. Upon entering the building, the way to the underground vault was immediately to my left: a spiral staircase led the way down. That first room itself was large and open. The hardwood floors were old and there was a chest on display extracted out of a safety deposit box after sitting unclaimed for over one hundred years. The chest was handcrafted, ornate and detailed. In contrast, there was also a modern piece of artwork in the room. Add in the Bourne Identity doors and you get old meets modern.

To get below ground all I had to do was walk down the little spiral staircase to the left of the front door. Seriously. If you are ever in Zurich, peak through the glass front doors and you can see it. I walked down one or two stories and entered a small room with a desk and two people sitting behind it. The room was bland and the people were not amused by any of my fellow associates. The employees behind the desk reminded me of the Goblins at Gringots. Pale and precise. The two people behind the desk wouldn't let us pass through the door at the other end of the room. That was it. We got to go underground and see the room that led to the rich stuff, but that's all. No gold. No treasure. No secrets. I was slightly disappointed, but at least it kept the dream alive. If I could actually get in the vault, then how special could it possibly be? I got to imagine the jewelry, secret documents, cash, weapons, ancient relics, and gold all stashed for safe keeping under Paradeplatz before going back upstairs.

The rest of the tour was through meeting rooms and offices – old rooms with modern furnishings and art. It said that Credit Suisse is old and conservative, but innovative at the same time. It said that this furniture is expensive but looks like Ikea.

After the tour, all the new associates went out to dinner with Andreas Iten, who ran the Credit Suisse Business School. I thought the dinner was amazing, but everyone else complained about it. We ate at Zunfthaus Zur Wag, one of the best guild houses in Zurich. Guild houses are the places you go to if you want traditional Zurich food: chopped meat with kidney, sliced veal or fresh fish from the lake with wine made from grapes grown on the shores of Lake Zurich. People complained that our room, with massive windows and wooden shutters opened so we could overlook Fraumunster square, was too hot and there was no air conditioning: the house was built in 1636. The floors were creaky: again 1636. Some in my training class also complained that there was too much food and wine and the two hours of dining was far too long. I, myself, was in heaven. I'll always look back on that meal as one of the best in my life.

The second night of dining was at Belvoir Park, the historic home of Alfred Eischer, founder of Credit Suisse. The fact that the restaurant was once home to Alfred Eischer was not lost on me. It wasn't published in any of our materials, but I came upon the information when doing some research prior to the dinner. Even if it hadn't been planned, even if it was a coincidence, I was happy to have picked up on it. The first day was a tour of the bank that Eischer built. The second night was a dinner at the house that Eischer built. The house had been converted into a French restaurant and was also the home of the Zurich School for Culinary Arts. The restaurant was a few blocks off the southern edge of

Lake Zurich. It was an enormous beauty in a neighborhood of behemoth old money mansion awesomeness. Our group walked through the dining room to our tables in the back garden overlooking the pond. White and pink flowers and pollinating bees painted the scene.

I sat next to Christian Machette, the head of all Human Resources who reported directly to Brady Dougan, CEO of Credit Suisse. We drank wine and chatted about nothing in particular. "Where did you go to school?" "Where are you from?" "How's the wine?" "How are you liking Zurich?" Much more European vacation than business. Questions such as, "How are you going to make money?" never came up. They never would. Making money was the one thing I had to do, but the one thing that no one knew how to do. Besides, "get lucky" made for a short training program.

So, we ate and drank and the one thing I did learn that night was that Belvoir Park puts out an amazing dessert table. That was the beauty of the restaurant. Instead of each associate having to pick our own dessert, Belvoir Park made an entire table of about twenty desserts for us. The pastry chef himself, who looked like a cherub with skin made of flour, butter and sugar, described each dessert to us. Since this was basically a lesson in rich extravagance, I indulged and made a game out of it.

I would do what I thought the very rich would do. I had one of each and pestered the waiter for more wine and more wine and more wine. I went back for seconds of the chocolate mousse and then thirds. You really haven't had chocolate mousse until you've been to Switzerland. Holy fuck it's good. No dessert compares to good chocolate mousse and Belvoir Park is the best I've ever had. I tipped my glass to Alfred Eischer and Brady Dougan and slowly walked back to my hotel. I Skyped my wife and went to sleep/food and wine coma.

The next day would be filled with more eating and impressive people. However, this day would be my chance to meet the most impressive of them all, Walter Berchtold, the head of Credit Suisse private banking for the entire world and the quintessential private banker of all time.

Walter Berchtold looks like Aaron Eckhart, but much more handsome and dashing with a chin that could take a punch. Just think to yourself European playboy and you will get a rough image of him in your mind's eye. Tanned. At home in one of his many high performance race cars tearing ass through the Swiss Alps as he is in a conference room full of suits or a billionaire client's yacht.

Maybe that was who Credit Suisse wanted me to become: little Berchtold. He gave what I imagine was a canned speech, which he had given time and time again, but all the associates hung on his every word. He was the man. Our leader. We would go into battle for him. Every woman in the room would have slept with him. We asked him a bunch of boring questions each pertaining to our own country. His answers made us feel like jerks or idiots, but we loved every minute of it.

My question to Berchtold was, "Do you think UBS should sell off its Dean Witter retail brokerage because it is not 'high net worth' and dilutes the brand?"

"That's a question for Ossie Grubal," Berchtold said with a smile.

Ossie Grubal used to be Berchtold's boss and is now CEO of UBS. You could tell Berchtold was happy Grubal was stuck with its crappy Dean Witter brokerage and its tax fraud lawsuit from the United States government. You could see it through his smile.

My final night of what I thought of as Credit Suisse's three days of lavish meals and impressive people in hopes of me early on experiencing what it was like to be very rich was at a little restaurant up in the hills overlooking Zurich. I didn't eat too much that night or sit next to anyone important. I didn't talk too much and just kept to myself drinking glass after glass of wine and slowly, over the course of a couple hours, got drunk. No one really knew. I kept it to myself, but I got hammered. I just sat there completely happy with myself and stared at the Swiss countryside. The next day would be Saturday and we had our weekends free. On Monday I would be given a case to work on with a team and would have to sit in class eight hours a day and take mandatory tests with scores that would be sent to my manager. However, that night I would act like a rich bastard and watch the Swiss rolling hills in a drunken haze from my dining room seat wearing my nicest suit.

Chapter Nine

Zur Oepfelchammer

On the first night of eating on my own, I discovered a place that I
will never forget. It was Saturday and after spending most of the
day studying, I left the hotel with plans to go to a restaurant I had
heard about called Zur Oepfelchammer. Outside of the hotel, I ran
into a group of guys from my training class who didn't know
where they wanted to eat. "Follow me." I said. "I think you will
love this place."

Zur Oepfelchammer is located just off Niederdorf Strasse, a
street full of restaurants and taverns: a restaurant row. Take a few
steps east off Niederdorf onto a narrow curvy street called
Rindermarket and you will run into Zur Oepfelchammer.
Originally built in 1357 as a townhouse in the cattle market, Zur
Oepfelchammer was turned into a pub/restaurant in 1801. It is
ancient and slightly off the beaten path. When I took my associate
class there, we walked up the steps of the townhouse and into the
dining room, most everyone said, "Ohhhhhh…this is cool." It's a
room that just does that to people. Even the most serious guy in my
class, a banker from Dubai who got his MBA at Oxford, told me I
did a good job picking out the restaurant. The guy never smiles,
but he had a good time that night.

The dining room is made entirely of oak. Oak walls, oak floors,
oak ceiling, oak tables. And, it is small. 25' x 40' with low
ceilings. Only four long tables with benches fill the room. My
favorite part about the restaurant is that every square inch of the
wood has names carved into it. Imagine name carvings on every
inch of the ceiling, walls and tables with only the floors spared.
That's the part that makes people say, "Ohhh…this is cool." For
hundreds of years, people have been getting drunk and carving

their names into this tiny room. It's not easy to get the right to carve your name into the dining room. You have to complete a challenge. I knew about this challenge and it was the reason why I led my classmates there.

The challenge involves the two massive twenty-five foot wood beams that run across the width of the dining room. The beams are about two feet below the ceiling. I'm 5' 10'' and I can reach up and put my hand on the top of them. If you can jump and hoist yourself onto the first beam then reach to the next beam and lay belly down across them, an old Swiss man comes from out of the kitchen with a full glass of white wine. If you can then hang your head over the second beam and drink the glass of white wine while upside down without spilling a drop, you can carve your name into the wood.

I like to think that our table was exactly what Brady Dougan, CEO of Credit Suisse, had hoped for when he created the Global MBA Private Banking Program. At our table were associates who would work out of the Zurich, New York, Dubai, London, and Madrid offices. And, of course me from Atlanta. It wasn't a bad showing – seven of the twenty-six new MBA hires from around the world. I picture Brady in his office overlooking Paradeplatz, literally standing over all the bank's underground vaults. I imagine him thinking that the ultimate culmination of his decision would be high powered MBAs from around the world sitting at an ancient Swiss table in Zurich, pounding the table with their fists, cheering on their new friends as they attempted the Zur Oepfelchammer challenge. Yes, we would sit through presentations and work on cases and compete to get the best scores on our tests. Brady is a trader from Chicago. He smokes like a chimney. I bet his best case scenario was all of us drinking and smoking cigarettes in this historic Swiss dining room pounding the table with the local Swiss citizens.

The first person to attempt the challenge that night was a big German guy that was sitting with some of his friends at the end of our table. You can only fit about twenty people max in this room. The German guy walked up to the beams and looked as if he was planning his strategy. As he was thinking, everyone started pounding the tables with their fists. It sounded tribal yet perfect for the occasion. As the German guy was studying the beams and all of us were pounding the tables, I looked around and couldn't help thinking how perfect the scene was. There were a couple of guys sitting near the window smoking cigarettes, overlooking the street, pounding a small table nearby. The rest of us were at a long table sitting shoulder to shoulder each knocking on the table for a stranger to complete the challenge. My classmates and I were all strangers as well, but we were a group of people from around the world with one common interest: private banking. The German guy took two steps back and jumped. He didn't make it.

I thought it would be easy. After the big German guy attempted and failed, I wasn't so sure. Once dinner was over, I got up from our table and gave it a go. On cue, everyone pounded the tables with their fists. It was a quiet rumble that grew into a roar. I approached the wood beams and assessed the challenge. It didn't seem too bad. I stepped back, enjoyed the sound of everyone's fists on the tables, and jumped. The first thing that I noticed as my body hit the wood and I wrapped my arms around the beam was that the beam was wide. Wide enough that I couldn't get any leverage to pull myself up. And the space I had to pass through was narrow enough that I couldn't get my elbows through. I let go and dropped down to the floor. I was a bit sore and thought if I could just get my elbows through, then I could pull myself up. Again, up I went. And, again both elbows got stuck. This time I struggled a little more and tried to muscle my way up, but just didn't have enough leverage. I dropped back down with only some skinned up elbows to show for it. No wine. No name carving.

The thing with this challenge is that I should have known it was difficult. If it was easy, then the old man that emerges from the kitchen with the full glass of white wine would get tired of walking out to the dining room to give out free booze.

"Enough already… I'm tired and old and running out of wine," he would say.

Also, if it was easy, then everyone would do it. It would lose its specialness and no longer be considered a challenge. No one else from my class even tried to attempt the challenge. Maybe I made that big of a fool of myself. Maybe everyone thought if skinny me couldn't do it why bother. Maybe they saw that it was actually damned difficult. Later in the evening, some Swiss college kids came in and sat at the corner window table. One of them, who must have done it before, completed the jump like it was nothing. He looked like a fish the way he slid up and across to the second beam, drank the glass of wine upside down, and dismounted.

The more I thought about Zur Oepfelchammer, the more it became something bigger than just a restaurant. It had some kind of power, like an oracle. I tried to go back with my wife when she flew into town for my last week of training, but it was closed. What bar/restaurant is closed on a Monday night? It was like a sign that said, "You had your chance, W.E.. Oracle Closed." In my mind, maybe this restaurant was a portal for the Swiss Banking Gods to speak directly to me. I thought maybe I wasn't fit to be a Swiss banker because I didn't complete the challenge. I didn't dwell on it for too long. I had more challenges ahead.

CHAPTER TEN

Real Training

If those first three days in Zurich were about teaching the new associates to act like the very rich and indoctrinating us into a rich lifestyle, then it worked. I turned the rest of training into an extraordinary vacation that I could never afford.

Instead of being treated like salesmen with no clients, which is essentially what we were, we were treated like millionaire clients or the crown jewels of the bank. Of the fifty-two thousand employees at Credit Suisse, we were a special twenty-six. We were the only brand new private banking associates from around the globe. We were important. We were entitled. We were pampered. We were different. If not for our Hugo Boss suits and Tumi briefcases, someone might have confused us with trust fund kids that the bank was trying to impress.

And we acted like spoiled trust fund kids. Each of us did it in our own way, but we were absolutely spoiled brats. When we started to act like spoiled brats, our personalities started to come out. The big, hearty (fat) Americans would complain, "What I have to include my $20 breakfast at the hotel as part of my $80 per diem? That's ridiculous. I need my $20 breakfast and it's technically not being charged to my AmEx. I'm charging it to my room. Come on!" The competitive athletic types would complain, "You are going to cover my gym membership, right? I need a workout and a hot tub before going to bed. After a long day I need my soak. I've got to have my soak!"

It was the middle of the Great Recession and we felt entitled. Personally, I would find my own way to rich it up. I never complained, I just lived it up and felt like I was getting away with something. I'm sure I didn't spend as much money on my corporate card as some, but I got after it in my own way-- through food and wine. Each night I would dine at some of the best restaurants in Zurich and went back multiple times to my favorites: Kindli, Hiltl, Il Giglio, Bodega Espanola, Restaurant Bederhof, Caduf's Wine Loft, Spruengli, Almodo Bar, Enigmatt, Weisses, Metropole, Mere Catherine. Hanging out with Caduff himself and picking out a bottle of 2006 Pingus, or gorging myself at Michelin star rated Il Giglio, I was doing my best to enjoy myself in my own way. To continue the Fitzgerald allegory, yes, I thought I was better than everyone because I was eating better. Other people would tell me where they ate at night and I would laugh to myself. You went there? I would also fly my wife in for a week and take her on a weekend vacation to Bellagio on Lago di Como. If Credit Suisse wanted to spoil me, I would play along.

A lot of personalities developed during real training. I won't go in to all twenty-six of us, but I will highlight those worth highlighting. The first and funniest is most undeniably a bloke I will call London City. He is obviously British. London City is the type of British that revels in being British. He was so proud and proper that it surpassed ridiculous. I'll give you an example. As tends to happen in private banking, our teacher asked us who the largest private landowner was in the UK. My friend, LBS, a Brit himself, answered Richard Scott. The answer was correct. However, London City, in all his proper Brithishness bellowed, "Lord Scott!" The truly British love their class system and London City wanted to make sure we all knew that he chose to refer to Richard Scott as "Lord Scott!" Richard Scott has about a million titles including, but not limited to, Earl, Baron, Marquis, Viscount, and Duke. I honestly do not know how one gets so many titles. Lots of political posturing hundreds of years ago is my guess. None the less, London City liked the title Lord the best.

It took about five seconds for the Irish guy sitting next to me, INSEAD, to pick up on this and go into a routine of joking around with London City in all his properness. I would say, "INSEAD have you ever heard of Darth Vadar?" Then INSEAD would reply, "Lord Vadar!"

The great thing about London City was that he knew we were making jokes, but didn't care because he was 100% sure that he was smarter and better than everyone because he was British. I have to admit, the bloke was very smart and a bit of a know it all, but I could tell straight away that he would be good at his job.

One exercise during training that truly highlighted London City was our morning speeches. Every morning one of the new associates would have to stand up in front of the class and do a market summary or teach the class something. It was a way to break the ice and get us comfortable speaking in front of people. London City, who had a background in wine and had worked for the largest wine merchant in the UK, was a massive wine snob and told the class a story about the best bottle of wine he ever had. It was a White Burgundy and he described it and the vintner at length. It was actually quite a good story. When it came to Q & A, the first question someone asked was, "How much is that bottle worth?" London City's answer was classic. He replied, "Priceless. I drank the last bottle." That was how full of himself London City was. He wouldn't say how much it was worth before he drank the last bottle, but since he, London City, wiped it out of existence it was priceless. Awesome. He might as well have said, "Priceless. I invented it in my mind and it doesn't exist." It was utterly ridiculous, but also great because it was coming from London City. I still have no idea how much that wine really cost. I couldn't get him to budge off of "priceless."

London City would be fiercely competitive during our team finance trivia contests we would have at the end of the day and he would get good scores. If the professor would say, "I can draw this option payoff diagram in less than five seconds and you should too," then London City would be the one timing the professor and then telling him, "Sorry...you were off by one second." A total know it all.

Another example of a big personality in our class was someone I will call Oxford Dubai because he went to school at Oxford and would be working out of the Dubai office. One of my first encounters with Oxford Dubai was when he asked me if I was married.

I said "Yes."

He then asked, "Does your wife cook?"

I said, "Yes."

To which he responded completely straight-faced and serious, "Good. That's the way it should be."

Once I figured out his love of subjugating women, I had a little fun with it. Before my wife flew into Zurich for a week, I told him that she was flying in and doing my laundry. "Of course. This is what women are for," he responded. My wife actually never does my laundry.

Oxford Dubai was extremely opinionated, smoked a ton of cigarettes and never smiled. He dressed like a rich Middle Eastern guy and thought everyone else around him was stupid. You see, that was the difference between him and London City. London City thought that London City was smarter, while Oxford Dubai thought everyone else was just dumber. When Oxford Dubai would speak in front of people and they didn't agree or understand what he was talking about, he didn't care because he just assumed they were dumb. He was dry and straightforward and didn't care what anyone thought.

The one person that truly was a genius but wouldn't tell you and really didn't talk too much was INSEAD Singapore. He went to INSEAD and would be working in Zurich. On weekends he would typically be partying somewhere in Europe with his friends. During the weekdays in training he would put his hands in his pants and sleep all through class and snore with his head falling backwards. Then, if there was some impossible question that no one could answer, INSEAD Singapore would raise his hand and answer as if it was the easiest thing in the world and he wasn't just snoring. He did this several times until it just became his thing.

UVA was the last of the big stand out personalities. He would take pictures of INSEAD Singapore sleeping or INSEAD Singapore with his hands down his pants or LBS Italy picking his nose. UVA was the clown who loved to take pictures of people doing dumb things in class: it happened a lot. He was that fast talking trader type guy. He wanted to be a trader. When he couldn't get a job as a trader, he took a job in private banking because it was the middle of the recession and MBA placement rates were getting crushed. Most everyone in the class was married and some even had kids, but UVA was a single guy wanting to live the life that everyone had heard of in fast paced Wall Street training programs. Lots of clubbing and picking up girls. He was always wanting to "go out." Unfortunately, Zurich is not the go out and pick up chicks kind of town. It's very quiet and calm. He would get frustrated that he couldn't pick up girls and that there weren't any good clubs. Fast talking guy on the prowl in Zurich was not a good combo. If he knew any better, he would have tried to hit southern Italian border cities for hot college girls. Lagano, for instance, would have given him what he was looking for. Lagano is where he should have been. The Greek in him would have fit in well with the Italian influenced culture down there.

I know you are thinking, "Well, what about the women?" I think private banking would be great for women, but it just wasn't happening in my associate class. There were only a few women. There was University of Chicago girl who you will hear about later. There was NYU girl who was a workout freak, always trying to get the group together to play sports, but it never happened because we were all lone wolf types that didn't like doing things in groups. She wouldn't last long. She would go on to work on the biggest team at Credit Suisse in the United States and only last a couple of months before leaving: not bringing in one client. There was Russian Girl who would work on the Russian desk in Zurich, but after a couple weeks on the job everyone found out she couldn't write in Russian and had to be moved. Finally there was an extremely quiet girl, INSEAD Girl, who would work in Zurich and never spoke a word to anyone other than to complain to the head of our program that Oxford Dubai offended her.

Everyone else in the program were good quiet people that did their work and had wives and children or were having them during training. We kept to ourselves and never went out in big groups too often.

When it comes down to it, private bankers are lone wolves. I-bankers are nerds, traders are meatheads and private bankers are lone wolves. We really don't work with anyone else. The most interaction I would have with any other private banker in my office was, "Hi, how are you." They would respond "Good" and that's it. I would open up my accounts. They would open up their accounts. We actually hate each other because we are competitors. We offer the exact same things to the exact same people. And we couldn't wait to see the other person get fired so we could steal some of their accounts. We are paranoid around each other and don't want anyone to know anything about our business. Even in the training program, we embraced this culture and played our cards close to our chest.

I think this is a personality that is attracted to private banking. Neurotic lone wolves. People who are competitive and don't like working with others. Think about it, our job is to put together a list of names that are our network and prospects and get those people to open accounts so we get credit for it. We don't want the other private bankers to know who is on our list. It's very private. Private and suspicious succeeds in this business. We don't need to work with anyone in our associate class because we all work in our own little world. So, who cares if I don't work well or want to build a relationship with another associate? I'm never going to need to work with them ever again. In fact, they are my competitor. I want to do better than them. So, it creates an interesting dynamic. Whereas I-bankers and traders might want to party with one another, it's nearly impossible for private bankers to come together as a group. Private bankers are far too secretive. It would be like James Bond and Jason Bourne going out drinking with George Smiley. No way. Those guys drink alone.

Chapter Eleven

My First Client

My first client's name was Michael Davies. He wasn't a cold call
or someone I already knew or a family friend. He was referred to
me by a mutual friend. When we were first introduced, Michael
was a dream prospect. He had a $30 million portfolio and actually
needed some financial advice. Of his $30 million, $16 million was
locked up in restricted stock at his current company, Regent
Corporation. The other half of his assets were at three different
banks in various funds and he was hoping to consolidate banks.
Michael had a complicated family life. He was fifty-eight years old
with three children from a previous marriage and two children
from his current marriage. His youngest son from his first marriage
wanted him to finance an art gallery for $400,000. His youngest
son from his current marriage had just been diagnosed with autism,
and Michael wanted to set up a trust for this son to ensure his well-
being. Michael's second wife was interesting. When we were first
introduced, she was thirty-nine years old and was already shopping
for what she described as her "retirement compound." She had her
heart set on a property. The only problem was that it wasn't for
sale. According to her, she just had to have it. Michael was the
type of prospect that everyone looks for–a millionaire that wants
help. First, he wanted to diversify his holdings and look at options
to sell some of his current company's restricted stock so his wealth
wasn't so tied to one company. Second, he wanted some
investment advice. What did we think of the way HSBC was
investing for him and how would we manage the money? And
third, he needed some trust and estate advice to help with his
complicated family. Lastly, Michael wanted some advice on
managing his cash-flow. He had a salary of $3.2 million per year

and lived paycheck to paycheck. Michael wasn't much of a saver. Michael also wasn't much of a real person.

Okay, so Michael wasn't real and was actually part of the team case I would have to present at St. Peter's Forum. St. Peter's Forum was the name of the building where we would give our final case presentation. It is where Brady Dougan holds meetings and makes announcements.

The presentations were a big deal. From the looks of my welcome packet, everything led up to the presentations. They were to be held on our last day in Zurich and Robert Weissenstein would be in attendance. If Zur Oepfelchammer was an Oracle through which the Swiss Banking Gods spoke, then Robert Weissenstein was one of the actual Gods. He is the Chief Investment Officer of the private bank. He's the guy who is on CNBC: the face of the private bank. He's on Power Lunch every month smoothly handling questions from anchor Sue Herrera. His onscreen personality is one part charisma, two parts policy wonk. And, he was flying in from New York specifically to see our presentations. Heck with the Oracle, I would talk to God himself.

The Michael Davies case was the first time I was ever given information on someone's entire financial situation and told to figure it out. I was excited. Ideally, this is exactly what private banking is about: someone giving you all their complicated information and saying figure it out. People will pitch this concept in different ways. Some people will say that "my objective is to be your family's CFO." Others will say that they are like a family's "financial doctor." They will say that when you go to a doctor's office you have no problem sharing all your personal information and when speaking with your financial advisor, it should be the same. Those are just techniques, but the objective is the same. You want to get all of a family's information so you can give them the best advice and turn their financial life into a streamlined business. After doing this, then you want them to refer you to their friends. Even though it was just a case, apparently it was based on some real life data. It might seem a little far-fetched, but once I started to actually do the job and meet with real prospects, I learned that the Davies family wasn't all that unusual.

Michael Davies was in luck. He didn't just have me working for him; he had a team of Swiss bankers from around the world. There would be two other bankers from the States on my team: Northwestern-Chicago and NYU-New York. Plus, there would two international bankers: LBS and Russian Girl. Michael would truly have access to Credit Suisse's global footprint.

All of us had just graduated from an MBA program and were quite accustomed to working on case studies in teams, having done so for the past two years. We approached the case like good MBAs; we decided on a time for a quick first meeting where we would then determine how to divide and conquer.

My part of the case was monetizing restricted stock. It sounds like something you shouldn't be able to do because it is restricted, but there are ways to get around the restrictions. Restricted Stock is not very complex, it's just some stock that has a restriction around it that prevents the owner from selling it. The restriction is typically continued employment. A company's board of directors will give a CEO stock and say that the CEO can't sell it until the CEO has worked at the company three years. That's a restriction. It's supposed to incentivize the CEO to see that the company's stock performs well for the next few years. Of course, there are ways around the restriction and one way is called a Variable Pre-Paid Forward Contract. The name is much more intimidating than the thing itself. Banks will structure a contract with the CEO and say that the bank will give the CEO cash for stock today as long as the CEO promises to give the bank the stock when it becomes unrestricted. The bank will tell the CEO if the stock goes up during that time, then he can participate in some of the positive returns. On top of that the CEO doesn't have to pay taxes until he gives the bank the stock. Basically, he gets cash today and doesn't pay taxes for a few years.

That was my part of the case. Michael had $16 million in stock and my job was to structure and price a Variable Prepaid Forward then stand in front of important people and explain what I did.

I chose to use a Variable Prepaid Forward to monetize Michael's restricted stock for a few reasons. First, like I said earlier, it is tax deferred and allowed Michael to retain some upside. Second, it gave him immediate proceeds. And third, it hedged downside risk via the upfront proceeds. If the stock went down, Michael wouldn't participate in the downside because he was already locked in. The negative parts of the Variable Prepaid Forward were that the upside was capped at a certain percentage, and the proceeds were received on a discounted basis. All in all, I thought this helped Michael accomplish his goal of monetizing his restricted stock and diversifying his portfolio.

Over the course of our month in Zurich, my team and I would meet between classes or after classes in bars and hotel rooms to discuss our progress, structure of the presentation and help each other on our analysis. Almodo Bar was a favorite for my teammate LBS and I to go to. Springli for coffees and chocolate was another favorite for Northwestern-Chicago and NYU-New York and I to go to. For my part, I also worked with Credit Suisse's derivatives desk in New York to price the Variable Prepaid Forward. Michael had 500,000 shares trading at $32, or $16 million in restricted stock. I called Joe Leo on our derivatives desk, told him I was a new associate and he was more than happy to help me with a structure. He loved that I was Skyping him from Zurich at 11 p.m. Zurich time. We structured a seven-year VPF for Michael. On day one Michael would be advanced $21 on his $500,000 shares, or $10,500,000. In seven years Michael would deliver the stock and then pay taxes. If the stock had appreciated at all during the seven years, Michael would get to participate in its appreciation up to $45/share. If the stock went down over the seven years, he wouldn't owe Credit Suisse a nickel.

In addition to the VPF, my entire team helped each other on each section of the presentation. There were essentially four parts: Client Overview, Restricted Stock Monetization, Investment Strategy, and Trust and Estate Solutions. Since there were four sections and five of us, we made LBS the person that would give opening and closing remarks. He had the best accent of us all and was a good opener and closer.

The day before St. Peter's Forum, the leader of our Zurich training program would make each team do a rehearsal in front of her and a Zurich banker. They would then critique us before we presented for real. These presentations were just as important for her as they were for us. If we did a bad job in front of Weissenstein, then he was going to ask her what the hell she had been doing with us for the past month and why we just wasted his time. I bet she was just as nervous as we were. During my dry run, the Zurich banker's comment to me was "W.E., I have no comments for you. I quite enjoyed listening to you speak." Admittedly, I was really on that time.

The rest of Zurich training was spent learning material in class and then being tested: Economics, Investment Vehicles, Modern Portfolio Theory, Laws and Regulations. If an associate made a perfect score their name would be announced to the rest of the class. We were very competitive and no matter how boring we thought training was, we always wanted to win. There were never an abundance of perfect scores: usually two or three. I believe I racked up the most or tied for most. I didn't fail. Matlock would be the only person to fail. When an associate failed, their failure was reported to their manager and they had to retake the test.

Case studies and head-to-head competitions are what make private banking different from most Wall Street training programs. They are what make the training actually kind of exciting. In addition to getting my name announced when I got a perfect score, I would also have to perform competitive mock calls in front of the entire class. It's the public humiliation that is more prevalent in private banking training than in investment banking training or sales and trading training. Private banking deems being able to communicate effectively as important. While trying to perform at your best, the entire class would be watching you. Under those circumstances, it didn't matter what school you went to, you could make yourself look dumb quickly and people would forget your GMAT score in a hurry if you sounded unintelligent speaking in front of a group.

I would also get to go on one last absurd dinner. This time it wasn't as fancy as the first few. This was a dinner tour of Zurich by trolley. After training one night all of the associates met in front of Paradeplatz 8 and an ancient trolley showed up, running on lines parallel to the ones normal trams ran on every day. The trolley must have been from the early 1900's. It looked like the diner car of an old locomotive. Everyone in Zurich was staring and pointing at us when we got on this thing. Dinner, wine, dessert, everything was served in the trolley car as it took us all over Zurich: even to the far off parts that I had never been to. Everywhere we went, people would stare. It must not have been a popular thing to do because people acted like they had never seen it before. We would stop, go on a little walk, get back on the trolley and drink some wine waiting for the next stop all the while trying not to spill food on our suits. It was like an embarrassing trip that parents make their children take against their will, but it made the whole training all the more unique.

CHAPTER TWELVE

Saint Peter's Forum

Saint Peter's Forum, or as the white lettering on the windows off
the sidewalk of Sankt Peterstrasse read "Forum St. Peter." This is
how the facility is described on the Credit Suisse website:

> "Welcome to the Forum St. Peter, Credit Suisse's best
> equipped Communication Center, right at the heart of
> downtown Zurich. Our aim is to contribute to the success
> of your event. We will therefore offer you professional
> advice during the preparation of your event and, if required,
> personal support during the event itself. The facilities
> include a foyer for hosting buffet lunches and drinks
> receptions, an auditorium for 200 people, two conference
> studios, as well as a variety of conference rooms with
> flexible seating and range of audio visual media."

On the morning of the Final Presentation, all twenty-six of us
arrived at Saint Peter's Forum with a huge sense of anxiety. I was
greeted in the foyer by the head of the training program and
chatted with my team as I watched Credit Suisse bigwig after
Credit Suisse bigwig enter the room. I was anxious to meet
Weissenstein and impress him. I knew this was a one of the most
important parts of training. First of all, the bank was flying in
Weissenstein specifically to watch the Case Studies. He would take
a taxi from the airport to St. Peter's Forum, watch the presentations
and then take a taxi back to the airport and fly back to New York.
That was it. Even though the woman running the training program
made us do a rehearsal and critique the day before our
presentation, no amount of rehearsal could have saved her from the
embarrassment she was about to experience.

I made awkward small talk with my friends and introduced myself to a few of the people that were there to judge my performance. There were about thirty people there to critique the presentations, but the only person that mattered was Weissenstein. As all of the associates left the foyer and walked into the auditorium there was still no sign of Weissenstein. This was the first time I was in the auditorium and my immediate reaction was that the setting was going to be a difficult one in which to perform. I was to stand on stage and address people sitting below me. I was to wear a microphone that echoed off the back wall as I spoke and made it very difficult to gage the sound of my voice. My presentation would be projected onto a massive white wall behind the stage and I would be filmed. The first team took its place on stage and got organized as we all waited for Weissenstein to show up.

Weissenstein was the last one seated in the auditorium, just off of the plane. As soon as he sat down, he laid his head back and closed his eyes. Team One began their presentation. The man that all of us wanted to impress, the man who we worked all month to present to closed his eyes and paid no attention to the team onstage. I thought he must have gone to sleep.

As each team member spoke from Team One it became obvious to me that the presentations were going to be fairly boring with people sounding nervous because they didn't want to mess up in front of the other associates and wanted to impress senior management. Add in the awkward setting and echo off the back wall and it turned everyone into monotone bores. It was pretty much a disaster. It proceeded as most business school presentations proceed. There would be a brief introduction followed by the words "Now I'd like to hand it over to so and so." Then, some more, "I'd like to hand it over to so and so's," until we got to The Awesomely Greatest Part of Any Associate Training Program Ever.

The Awesomely Greatest Part of Any Associate Training Program Ever began with the words, "Now I'd like to hand it over to University of Chicago Girl." University of Chicago Girl is one of those people that make you wonder how the hell did that person make it into the University of Chicago. How the hell did she make it into the private banking associate program? How the hell did she make it out of bed this morning without hurting herself? How was she even able to walk down the road and know what streets to turn down to get to the University of Chicago? The girl graduated from one of the best finance schools of all time, yet didn't know what a derivative was. She didn't even pass her Series 66 when we had to get licensed. At the time, I knew University of Chicago Girl was a bit slow, but I had never seen her speak in front of people and just thought she must have great communication skills. Nope.

She began her presentation by fucking up the remote that advanced the PowerPoint slides. She hit the button too many damn times and it advanced three slides ahead of where she wanted to be. She had to go to the computer, exit out of the slide show and go back a couple slides, all while muttering things like "Sorry " and "Hold on." By the time she got everything fixed, I could see the terror in her eyes. She hadn't said a word and had already fucked up big time. She was completely off her game. That is assuming she had some semblance of game. She forgot what to say. She spoke about nothing that could be confused as intelligent and then cut herself short and said, "Now, I'm going to turn it over to so and so." She handed so and so the remote and as she was walking back to her chair on stage she passed out. Yes, passed the fuck out. She slipped. She banged her head on the wall that the slides were being projected upon. She came back to consciousness and stumbled a little. I heard the entire audience gasp in shock thinking she would fall off the stage.

"Hhhhhhhahhhhh." Everyone held their breath.

She came to quickly, barely regained her balance and sat down in her chair on stage. Holy what the fuck, you've got to be kidding me. No matter the language, German, Swiss, Spanish, Arabic, Farsi, English, Russian, that was what was on everyone's mind. No one felt sorry for her. It was a competition and she was supposed to perform at a very high level. She couldn't mess up that bad. She just couldn't.

Don't worry, The Awesomeness is not over. As the next person on her team was giving their spiel, University of Chicago Girl stood, walked off stage, busted through the double doors exiting the auditorium and puked everywhere. She then slipped and fell in her own vomit. The last thing I saw before the double doors swung shut was University of Chicago Girl on all fours sitting in her throw up. Doors closed.

No one knew how to react at first. What just happened? There's no way that just happened, right? The people on stage didn't really know what happened and just kept presenting. I thought to myself, "Okay. If you said to me what's the worst that could happen to you during your presentation, I would have thought maybe I would forget a few lines. No way would I ever have thought that sitting in my own throw up was an option." A girl walked out of the auditorium and helped University of Chicago Girl. The woman that was running the program didn't even get up to help her. That's how hardcore and intimidating these presentations were. The team onstage finished its presentation and it was time for audience Q&A. Guess what? University of Chicago Girl was back! She cleaned herself up and came back for Q&A. Q&A was Weissenstein's opportunity to grill us and make our analysis seem like a joke. He didn't give a fuck and he attacked University of Chicago girl. It was phenomenal. I don't know how he knew as much as he did. Maybe he was a god because he had his eyes closed the entire time and knew every number and comma in the entire presentation. There was a problem with University of Chicago Girl's numbers adding up on one of her slides and he caught it even with his eyes closed.

"Can you add these numbers for me?" Asked Weissenstein.

"Sure…oh…it's a mistake. That's not what the number should be."

"Then why did you put it there?"

"It's a mistake, I'm sorry."

"You can't make mistakes. I don't care what it says in the rest of your presentation. Since that number is wrong, the whole thing is probably wrong. Did you even bother to proofread this?"

"I'm sorry it's just that…"

"Next."

My team was next and it was impossible not to feel the tension in the room. The first group was so bad it just threw everyone off. My group and I huddled in the back of the room and gave ourselves a pep talk to try to bring some good energy to the stage. LBS did a great job with opening remarks and handed it over to NYU New York who would do an acceptable job given that English wasn't his first language. I could tell we were starting to lose the audience. I was next after NYU New York. I got up from my seat on stage, he handed off the Power Point clicker, and I walked up to the podium. There was absolutely no energy coming from the audience. I looked over to Weissenstein and he had his eyes closed. I stepped to the side of the podium with hopes of increasing my ability to connect and speak directly to the audience without hiding behind the big wooden object. It helped a little, but I still didn't feel a great connection. I went through the motions because I had everything in my head down pat, but it felt very flat. At least I got the information out without throwing up on myself. The presentations were built up to be so big and important that when I actually got up on stage to speak and the vibe from the audience was essentially "let's get on with it, I want to go back to work," it just threw me off. It didn't help that the other teams were hoping beyond hope that I would fail. As soon as I sat down from doing my part I felt sad that it was over and I wasn't spectacular. I gave a boring presentation. My team covered all the bases but we didn't nail it and our flow seemed off. The best part of our presentation was Q&A. All of the little things that make a speaker pop that were missing from my part of the presentation, I brought into Q&A. Weissenstein would interrogate each team member on their part and no one ever won. I put up a good fight.

"W.E, why did you choose a Variable Prepaid Forward as opposed to some other strategy?"

"I considered alternatives like a Zero Premium Collar and Purchasing Put Options, but Put Options are very expensive and require a large outlay of cash. The Zero Premium Collar would have not given Michael any upside appreciation. The Variable Prepaid Forward truly gave Michael everything he wanted: upfront proceeds so he could diversify, hedged his downside and gave him some upside if the stock appreciated over the seven years."

"Where did you get these prices?"

"I called Joe Leo on the Equities Derivatives Desk and worked with him to arrive at the pricing."

"When are taxes paid?"

"Taxes are paid in seven years when Michael delivers the stock to Credit Suisse."

"Are these qualified or non-qualified options?"

"The case didn't state what type of options they are."

"That's no excuse. When working on these cases you have to ask questions, and not knowing whether these are qualified or non-qualified is important. The tax implications are completely different. You need to know this. Next."

The only thing any of us could do during Q & A was to just keep the ball in play for as long as possible. Eventually we would lose and Weissenstein would win.

Even the big personalities couldn't pull off a good presentation. London City, who knows everything about the bank and is actually a very good speaker, looked terrified. I could tell that the echo he was getting off the back wall made London City self-conscious about his voice. UVA, the fast talker, talked even faster and sweated through his shirt because he got so nervous. He just motor mouthed and sweated his way through his portion. INSEAD Zurich, who was a boy genius and slept through everything, played it best and acted like he really didn't care about the whole thing and only spoke for a couple of minutes. Matlock was only allowed to introduce the family and not talk about numbers. Oxford Dubai sounded particularly bad and unpolished, but I'm sure in his mind he was perfect. My favorite presenter was my buddy INSEAD Ireland. Like me, he stood off to the side of the podium and I thought he connected with the audience. After the presentation, he said, "You Americano's are all great presenters. I like how you stood off to the side of the podium. It was like Steve Jobs. That's why I did it." It worked for him. He was the best of the group. Don't worry, his team still got hammered by Weissenstein.

Even though I didn't perform well, the experience itself was truly impressive. I was a Swiss banker sitting in St. Peter's Forum, where the CEO, Brady Dougan, gave his addresses. We were teams assembled from around the world and I would never work on such a glamorous client or presentation again. Even though I felt like a lamb being led to the slaughter, I was slaughtered by Robert Weissenstein, the guy that is always on CNBC. At least the person giving me a hard time was one of the most famous people at the bank. At first I felt awful, but then I realized that the experience was supposed to make me tougher and I felt proud that I made it.

All of us filed out of the auditorium into the foyer where there was cake and coffee waiting for us. This was our last day and the last time I would get to see a lot of my new international friends. I said my goodbyes and then as I was about to leave to begin packing, I noticed a lot of people taking pictures of the cake with their phones. No one in my associate class had shown nearly as much interest in food as me, so I was very curious as to why they were taking pictures.

The cake was an absolutely perfect photo realistic copy of Paradeplatz 8. It was from Springli, arguably the best chocolatier in the world.

"Apparently, the cake cost $500." A fellow associate said to me.

"$500!" I said.

Just when I thought my Zurich food indulgences were coming to an end, Credit Suisse went and bought me a $500 cake that was an absolute perfect rendering of Paradeplatz 8. I had to have a piece, but in my mind I had to have the best piece. I looked at the cake. I marveled at it actually. When the caterer began slicing pieces I made up my mind and pointed to the piece that I wanted. The best piece. Brady Dougan's office!

I spent my last night packing and going out on the town. My wife was still in Zurich and we went out to bars with most of the associate class. We walked past Zur Oepfelchammer that night. The oracle was closed. I really wanted to try the challenge again before leaving Zurich, but it wasn't meant to be. My wife and I had a nice quiet dinner at Kindli together. It was a parting dinner for us. The next day she would fly to Atlanta and I would fly to New York for the final month of training before the real job began.

CHAPTER THIRTEEN

One Madison, Eleven Madison

Credit Suisse's New York headquarters are located at One Madison Avenue and Eleven Madison Avenue. They are right next to each other and connected by a skywalk on an upper floor. One Madison was the largest building in the world from 1909 to 1913. It is fifty stories tall, designed by the architectural firm Napoleon LeBrun, and modeled after the Campanile in Venice, Italy. It is an iconic New York building overlooking Madison Square Park with its clock tower looming above. Even today, over one hundred years since it was first built, it is still easy to pick out of the New York skyline when flying into the city.

Next to One Madison is Credit Suisse's other building Eleven Madison. It is only thirty stories tall, but at the time of its construction it was intended to be one hundred stories tall and the tallest building in the world. The building was designed by Harvey Wiley Corbett and D. Everett Waid. As they were building what was to be the tallest building in the world, the Stock Market Crash of 1929 hit and they ran out of money stopping at only thirty floors. The base of the building takes up an entire square block and gives the building a fat, stubby look of a skyscraper stopped short. It is more ziggurat than skyscraper. The interior of the building has an art deco feel to it and is now made famous by Danny Meir's restaurant Eleven Madison Park. Or, as my wife would later describe to me, "the place where Big tells Carrie that he is engaged in *Sex and the City*."

The New York portion of training was focused on passing the Series 66 and 7 and working on a case with Robert Weissenstein acting as the mock client. Day one of New York training found me in Robert Weissenstein's office with Matlock as my case partner. I wasn't thrilled. I was a little wounded from my last encounter with Weissenstein and knew that he was going to play tough with us for the rest of training. Weissenstein was running late for our meeting, so Matlock and I just waited in his office. Our case with Weissenstein would span an entire month and include one meeting and two presentations.

The first meeting was a test to evaluate our skills at gathering information from a prospect. The two presentations were supposed to be our attempt at solving the prospect's problems and opening a new account. For this first meeting, Matlock and I strategized on how to gather information and confirm a second meeting. Beforehand, we had decided on asking open-ended questions. Matlock would begin the discussion and ask questions about the prospect's family and estate planning. Then, I would ask questions about the client's portfolio and investment objectives. We already had a sheet with some of this information on it, but we needed to dig a little deeper to get a sense of how to structure our presentation in the second meeting.

The key thing to recognize here is that a large part of our training thus far had been on asking open-ended questions. It was sales 101. How have you been investing? What would you like the money to do? How would you describe your relationship with your current firm? How would you describe your estate plans? Tell me a little about your family and business. The whole point is to ask questions that the guy can't say "no" to. He's got to elaborate a little.

Waiting in Weissenstein's office was like waiting in the den of a lion that wanted to kill us. We weren't private banking associates. We were food. When Weissenstein arrived, he brought along one of the VP's on his team to act as his accountant. All of us introduced ourselves and then we began asking questions. We only got about five minutes with Weissenstein so we needed to get as much information as fast as possible.

Matlock, as planned, started asking questions in regard to the prospect's family. He asked, "How would you describe your family and estate plans?" It was a nice open-ended question and as the words were coming out of his mouth I just hoped Weissenstein would not play hardball with us.

Unfortunately, hardball was all we got and Weissenstein replied, "It's personal. I don't want to talk about that. I don't plan on dying any time soon." Matlock then turned red, shut down and didn't say another word for the rest of the meeting.

After Matlock froze, I stared at him and thought, "Are you kidding me? You're done? Don't you want to say anything else?" Nope. Silence. I scrambled because Matlock threw out the entire game plan. One question and he was out. So, I thought for a second and then started firing out questions and scribbling down notes to try to get some information on which to base our second meeting/presentation. I went right back with Trust & Estate questions because I knew that we needed some of that to be in the presentation and I didn't bother putting it in open ended question form. Weissenstein wasn't in the mood for chitchat open ended question stuff. So, I just went for an information grab with the four minutes we had left.

"Do you have wills?"

"Yes"

"When was the last time they were updated?"

"Follow up with my accountant."

"Have you ever done any estate planning or have any trusts established?"

"No."

"Would you like more information on trust and estate planning, perhaps in our next meeting?"

"Sure."

"What are your thoughts on the market right now?"

"I don't know, you tell me."

Wow…every open ended question was getting shot down.

"I noticed that a large portion of your portfolio is concentrated in large cap US stocks, would you like to see how we structure a diversified portfolio?"

"Sure."

"I noticed that you travel to China a lot, do you think favorable of the Chinese market?"

"Yes. I think there is going to be a lot of growth in China over the next several years."

"One last thing. Can you give the ages of each member of your family?"

"Follow up with my accountant."

"Great. I'll do that. Let's meet again and we can show you some information on trust and estate planning, and a diversified portfolio with some China investments included."

Done. Matlock was still frozen. It was like he wasn't used to not having everything come easy to him and actually having to work. This case was doomed. Weissenstein was going to kick our butts up and down Wall Street no matter what I did.

CHAPTER FOURTEEN

How Private Bankers Make Money

In addition to my time spent working on Weissenstein cases and taking Series 7 and 66 classes, the rest of New York training was spent with private bankers telling me their stories of how they got their clients and Credit Suisse professionals presenting me with the myriad of investments and services I could offer clients. This portion of training was great because I started to learn what I could offer to people.

In between presentations from Credit Suisse professionals, Eric Dale, the head of the training program, loaded a PowerPoint presentation onto the computer in our classroom. The presentation had two slides and he only spent two minutes on the slides. However, these turned out to be the two most important minutes of my two months of training. It went by so quickly that I grabbed my pen and paper and tried to jot down information as fast as possible. I alternated between writing and raising my hand. When not called upon, I just gave up and kept writing. What could possibly be so important? The slides were titled, "The Economics and Performance Goals for MBAs on Teams."

I knew that my job was to open up accounts and bring in new assets to the firm. I was to use my network and sales skills to bring money into the bank for me to invest. People would pay me a commission to invest the money for them. I knew all of this. I knew that I would get a salary of $95,000/year (now $100,000) for my first two years and that after my first two years I would live off of commissions only. The one thing that no one ever told me or anyone else in the associate class was how those commissions were calculated. Each of us had a vague notion of what the numbers were, but we were never given the actual math and an example.

On the first slide, it said that in year one, as a private banking associate, I was expected to bring in $20 million in new accounts for me to invest, which equated to $1.67 million per month. In year two I was expected to bring in another $20 million for a total of $40 million after two years. To help bring in the new accounts, I could work on teams with older private bankers in the office and they would share in all the new accounts that I brought in. My first year, I would get a $95,000 salary plus 15% of the commissions from my new accounts. The other 85% would go to whoever helped me bring in the account. If no one helped me open the account, the 85% would be kept by the bank. In my second year I would get $95,000 salary plus 25% of the commissions from my new accounts. The other 75% would go to a senior private banker or be kept by the bank. And, after my second year I would get 50% of the commissions from my new accounts and an initial split of the commissions of the team that helped me bring in my accounts and had been sharing in my revenues for the first two years.

So, let's do a math problem and figure this out. To help me with the math problem, the top of the slides told me to expect that my commissions should average 0.75% and that 35% of that will go to the new associate and the team.

At first it seemed a little confusing, but I whipped out my calculator and started punching in numbers. The first thing I did was to multiply $20 million by 0.75%. This equals $150,000 and is called my "revenue." Now, according to the slides, 35% of that revenue went to me and my team. The rest went to the bank.

So, the second step was to multiply $150,000 by 35%. This equals $52,500 and is the amount that would go to me and my team.

Finally, the slides said that during my first year I would get 15% of the money as a bonus and my team would get 85% of the money as a bonus. I multiplied $52,500 by 15%. My bonus for bringing in $20 million of new accounts my first year would equal $7,875. So, my total compensation for my first year, if I brought in $20 million would be $102,875.

Okay, that was year one. Now, let's figure out year two. The first thing I did was to multiply $40 million by 0.75%. The $40 million was from $20 million from my first year plus $20 million from my second year. This equals $300,000 in revenue. Again, 35% of this would go to me and my team. So, I multiplied $300,000 by 35%. This equals $105,000.

Finally, I multiplied $105,000 by 25%. My bonus for bringing in $40 million of new accounts over two years would be $15,705. Combined with my $95,000 salary my second year compensation would equal $110,705.

It's at this point in every private banking associate's career when things get interesting. Year three would be the year when I would live completely off of commissions.

Let's dive into it shall we? In year three let's assume that I bring in another $20 million. That will bring me up to $60 million in assets.

First step, I took $60 million and multiplied it by 0.75%. This gave me $450,000. I Multiplied that by 35% and got $157,500. Then, I multiplied that by 50% and my compensation in year three would be $78,750.

Once I got to that number, I raised my hand and Eric exited out of the PowerPoint presentation.

"Wait…hold on. Can you go back to that? If I bring in $60 million, I make less money?"

The answer was that in addition to the $78,750, your team would also let you share in some of the team revenues. Or, maybe they would let you keep a greater share of the $157,500. Basically, in year three you better do some good negotiating with your team.

If the senior private bankers didn't give me some of their revenue then I could bring in $60 million and still be screwed.

My general mood after seeing those slides was one of denial. I tried to ignore what they meant. I knew that the success rate was low. I had heard that only about one in twenty will make it past two years. There were only ten people in my class. This meant that perhaps every single one of us would be gone in two years. Seeing the numbers was a real eye opener and it helped me see the world of private banking a little more clearly.

I thought about the makeup of the Atlanta office. The youngest person in the office that wasn't on salary was thirty-nine and had been working at Credit Suisse for six years. There were no young MBAs in the office that were off salary. When I had taken the job I thought it was a good thing because I would be the only young guy in the office at the age of thirty-two. However, maybe it meant that I wouldn't make it to thirty-five and still be with the firm. I chose to focus on the positive aspects of the job. We were in the midst of the Great Recession and for two years I would be paid to try. And, that's what I would do: try. If I brought in $20 million my first year, I would get $102,875. If I brought in $0 my first year, I would still get $95,000. Like Paul Newman said, "sometimes nothin' is a cool hand."

Next, my thoughts went toward game theory. What if I brought in nothing for two years, then on my first day of my third year I brought in $60 million of accounts on my own and got to keep all the revenue? All things being equal, that was the best way to play the game. The worst way to play the game still wasn't so bad: $95,000 for two years in a recession for doing nothing and adding no value. When I thought about it that way, the difference between zero and $60 million didn't seem all that large.

My thoughts also went to variables that could predict success. If only one in twenty make it, I wondered if demographic or previous relationships skewed the success rate. Were people in New York and San Francisco getting a one in twenty success rate while perhaps Atlanta was more like one in fifty? Were people that already had connections and million dollar accounts committed to them before they even started the job more successful? Maybe instead of asking to pitch a stock in an interview, the question should be, "how many accounts will you bring in on day one," because if you don't bring in any accounts on day one chances are you won't make it. Maybe the performance of the market had an effect on success. The market had a negative annualized return over the past ten years! I was freaking out a bit. I don't know why but just seeing it in real number form and doing the math on my calculator did that to me. I decided that worrying wasn't going to help. I wasn't even going to have a job if I didn't pass my Series 7 and 66.

So, now you know how it works. It's not an exact science, but that formula is a good basis. Some of you might break out your calculators and start trying to back into how Jeremy Jones made $1 million his last year at Goldman and how long it will it take Credit Suisse to make up the $11 million they paid him. And, for those of you, all I can say is be patient, we'll get there but for someone like him the calculations are slightly different.

CHAPTER FIFTEEN

7 and 66

All new Associates working in Private Banking or Investment Banking have to take the Series 7. The Series 66 is exclusive to Private Banking and investing professionals. Even though everyone has to take the 7, both tests are truly only relevant to Private Banking. I never quite understood why my Investment Banking friends had to take the Series 7. It has absolutely nothing to do with their jobs and here's why. There are 17 topics covered in the Series 7. Of those, I consider only one absolutely essential to Investment Bankers: Issuing Securities and that topic will only entail 10-15 of the 250 total questions., The remainder of the test is really for Private Bankers with topics that include: Customer Accounts, Margin Accounts, Investment Company Products, Brokerage Support Services, Trading Securities, Recommendation Suitability & Taxation, Retirement Plans, Variable Annuities, Direct Participation Programs, Government and State Regulations which includes Cold Calling Rules, SEC and SRO Rules and Regulations, Economics and Analysis, Municipal Securities, Options, Debt and Equity. So you have to wonder why Investment Bankers are being tested on the rules surrounding opening New Accounts and rolling over IRAs?

As Private Bankers, it is much more essential to pass the exam on your first go round than it is for Investment Bankers. Investment Bankers think the test is a joke and some might not pass because none of them take the test seriously. Their boss isn't going to fire them for not passing the first time because their boss knows it has nothing to do with their job. If an Investment Banking Associate doesn't pass the Series 7 on the first go round, they can still work every day. Their group will give them financial modeling to work on or Pitch Books to make or research to do.

You can still work 12-hour days in Investment Banking and not have passed your Series 7. However, a Private Banking Associate is much different. The Series 7 has everything to do with your job. If you don't pass the Series 7, the only thing you can do at work is sit and stare at your computer and read the Internet. Don't think about touching a phone and talking about investments. Private Banking Associates take the Series 7 very seriously and study for it every day for a month. If you don't pass it, you are giving the bank a great excuse to kick you out of the training program.

This is how the Series 7 is broken down:

Prospecting for and Qualifying Customers	4% of the Exam
Evaluating Customer Needs and Objectives	2% of the Exam
Providing Customers with Investment Information and Marking Suitable Recommendations	49% of the Exam
Handling Customer Accounts and Account Records	11% of the Exam
Understanding and Explaining the Securities Markets Organization and Participants to Customers	21% of the Exam
Processing Customer Orders and Transactions	5% of the Exam
Monitoring Economic and Financial Events, Performing Customers Portfolio Analysis, and Making Suitable Recommendations	8% of the Exam

One thing that I love about the Series 7 is the Evaluating Customer Needs and Objectives part. I love it because for some reason it has made itself into practically every Wealth Manager's spiel on commercials on CNBC. I see so many commercials that say, we're different because we listen to our customers' needs and objectives. I always want to yell at the screen, "Actually everyone does that! It is so generic that it is on the Series 7. You know, the test that everyone in Finance takes. Actually, guy in commercial, it is the exact opposite of different."

These Wealth Manager commercials will also get into suitability. Suitability is something that gets a lot of talk in financial regulation these days. I've heard commercials that say, our advisors are held to a much stronger fiduciary duty and therefore you should trust us more than the other guy. All these commercials are doing is quoting a licensing exam. Everyone has some sort of suitable or fiduciary duty. For crying out loud, 49% of the Series 7 is on suitability. However, there's suitability and then there is fiduciary duty.

After passing the Series 7 you are considered a General Securities Representative or a "Stock Broker." As a General Securities Representative you are allowed to give advice that is suitable at the time that you give it only. This makes perfect sense to me because as a General Securities Representative, you are only allowed to make a commission: no ongoing fee based accounts. So, since you are only paid at the time of the transaction, you should only be responsible for giving suitable advice at the time of the transaction. So, a General Securities Representative, or Stock Broker, only has a suitability responsibility to you at the time that he sells you something.

When firms advertise that they have a greater fiduciary responsibility they are basically saying that they are Registered Investment Advisors and have passed their Series 66, which allows them to take a fee for giving long term advice – typically 1% per year. As long as you are paying the advisor, the advisor is responsible for fiduciary advice. If you are paying a 1% fee over the course of the year and your investment risk tolerance changes, making an investment wrong for you, then the advisor has a fiduciary responsibility to give you advice regarding it because you are paying him to do so. Basically, fiduciary responsibility is directly tied to the timing of payments to the advisor. A one-time fee equals a one-time suitability check. Fees over time equal fiduciary over time. That is the only difference between a "broker" and an "advisor."

Aren't Private Bankers and Private Wealth Managers a little different because they are supposed to be like Super Stock

Brokers? Well, yes. Most Private Bankers are what is known as hybrids. A hybrid works for a Broker Dealer, but is registered as both a Registered Representative and an Investment Advisor. Private Bankers just have to be a little fancier, so yes they are both. Today, typically all new hires take both the Series 7 and the Series 66. That's one of the reasons I say stockbrokers are dead. Another reason is just the way that people work these days. No one just sells you a stock any more. Here are some examples from various firm's websites:

Morgan Stanley Smith Barney Private Wealth Management

Since our inception, we have been dedicated to serving our clients through a relationship based on intimacy, integrity and mutual trust. When a new client comes to Private Wealth Management, our relationship begins with a discovery process--an in-depth dialogue to identify all the factors surrounding and defining the client's wealth. This includes the client's short and long-term goals and concerns, the structure of his or her holdings, and the client's exposure to–and tolerance for–risk. The client's dedicated team and wealth management specialists then work with the client to construct, implement and monitor an asset allocation strategy that will help the client achieve his or her many objectives

JP Morgan Private Banking

- Seek to deliver positive risk-adjusted returns appropriate to our clients' financial goals and risk tolerances.

- Provide an exceptional breadth and depth of wealth management solutions including investing, wealth structuring, capital advisory, philanthropy and banking.

- Leverage both J.P. Morgan-affiliated managers and third-party managers who are subject to rigorous ongoing due diligence.

- Communicate closely and regularly with clients to keep them constantly informed about the changing landscape.

- Compensate our advisors based on our clients' performance; no one is paid on commission.

Goldman Sachs Private Wealth Management

We evaluate each client's needs and preferences by determining spending and lifestyle requirements, anticipated large capital expenditures, philanthropic interests and desire for generational wealth transfer. Our process balances investment opportunities across geographies and among a wide range of asset classes. We employ an approach to asset allocation based on a robust quantitative framework that measures the trade-offs between risk and return. This enables us to provide the appropriate level of portfolio diversification. Throughout the year, we may recommend tactical shifts within a portfolio in order to capitalize on current investment opportunities. We develop a thoughtful, step-wise plan to implement the asset allocation best suited to a client's needs. Taking into account current market conditions and economic trends, we review each client's portfolio on an ongoing basis and evaluate possible adjustments.

Credit Suisse Private Banking

Our Relationship Managers work with you through a structured advisory process to produce the appropriate long-term strategy and investment choices for your profile.

Our Advisory Process has five steps:

Step 1: Needs analysis. Understand your needs and objectives.

Step 2: Financial concept. Develop a customized financial concept focusing on your assets and liabilities and cash flows.

Step 3: Client profile. Identify your readiness to take risks and your financial capacity to accept them.

Step 4: Strategy. Recommend an appropriate investment strategy.

Step 5: Implementation. Implement and monitor your strategy and manage your assets.

Northern Trust

We take the time to understand your individual goals and needs and create your investment portfolio using the best investment solutions for your situation.

1. Identify your goals. Identify liquidity needs. Assess tolerance for risk and discuss time horizon. Establish income targets. Review investment preferences.

2. Design your portfolio. Identify return objectives and ranges of volatility. Identify investment strategy. Set asset allocation. Determine performance benchmarks. Create investment policy statement.

3. Construct your portfolio. Conduct security and manager research. Construct diversified portfolios. Combine securities and managers in optimized proportions.

4. Manage your portfolio. Replace securities and managers that fail to meet objectives. Monitor continued compliance with investment guidelines.

GEEKS WHO CAN SCHMOOZE

5. Evaluate and discuss. Examine the market for new ideas. Monitor changing trends, market conditions and legislation. Communicate and discuss. Determine performance benchmarks. Adjust and adapt with your changing circumstances.

Those are all broker-dealers. Their workers are either "Registered Representatives" or "hybrids." And, like I said earlier, most new employees are going to be hybrids. I think it's safe to say that all of them do the same thing and basically quote the Series 7 back to us. To me, JP Morgan does seem to be the most different of them all, but all of them look at needs/goals and then they invest money. All of them say the exact same thing. None of them say that they pick great stocks. Could perhaps a Registered Investment Advisor say something different? A Registered Investment Advisor is not as easy to find as a broker-dealer. Even the smaller named firms around your town are probably broker-dealers. Typically Registered Investment Advisor companies will be started by people that leave a broker-dealer to start their own shop. In Atlanta, I found one called Hombrich Berg founded by a bunch of guys that left SunTrust bank. On the Homrich Berg's website it said that it was an "SEC-registered" investment advisor. Perfect! That's just what I was looking for. Here's what their website says:

> Homrich Berg offers a comprehensive approach to asset allocation, diversification and active asset management, taking into account each client's specific goals and risk tolerance and our outlook for capital markets, including domestic and international markets (e.g., stocks, bonds, hedge funds, real estate, commodities and private equity).
>
> Capital is managed in a flexible, personalized style. No two clients' portfolios are identical because of differing financial resources, objectives, tax considerations and tolerance for risk. We report quarterly to our clients on the allocation and performance of their investment capital. We provide a detailed analysis of a client's total financial

condition. A personalized strategy is designed to achieve the client's wealth management goals. Our financial planning services include the following: Estate Planning, Wealth Transfer Strategies, Strategic Philanthropy, Education Funding, Insurance Reviews, Income Tax Planning, Retirement Planning.

It's the exact same as all the rest. You have to ask yourself, does it really matter whether I give my money to a "Registered Representative" or a "Registered Investment Advisor" or a "Hybrid?" They all do the exact same thing. Supposedly one has a slightly higher legal standard. Do I really care about that or do I care more about me trusting one guy and to hell with all the marketing materials and registrations? Personally, I think it comes down to the client and the person sitting across the table from the client. Either the client trusts the advisor or not. At a corporate level they all sound the same. And, at a legal level they are virtually indistinguishable.

This is something that I thought about a lot as I was studying for my Series 7 and 66. Every night for a month I would sit in my class with Harvey Knopman training. He trains the entire Street and I would be just like all the other Private Bankers and Investment Bankers out there: another Registered Rep that passed his test because of Harvey Knopman. I would study in my own way. Each night after Knopman class I would sit at the bar of a restaurant, order dinner and study. I hit a lot of great restaurants this way. Casa Mono. Gramercy Tavern. Craft Bar. Bar Boloud. Bar Masa. WD50. MomoFuku. The Modern. Posto.

Over dinner and some wine my mind would start thinking about the type of Private Baker I would become. I would be a "hybrid," but I knew that what really mattered was not me passing a test for the SEC but my own values and knack for making money. Some people have values and some don't. Some people have a knack for making money and some don't. There's no way you can put that in a marketing campaign, so everyone just makes up the same five-step process and calls it unique.

I took my tests and passed them. First I took the 7 and then a week later I took the 66. These tests are all electronic and give you your score as soon as you are done taking them. As my 66 score appeared and said that I passed, a great sense of relief washed over me. I stood up from my testing station and looked around the room. Sitting behind me were two JP Morgan Investment Banking classmates of mine from Emory taking the Series 7. We caught eyes and I gave them a wave. Then, I smiled to myself because they were probably answering a question completely irrelevant to their careers like rules on 403-b retirement plans for teachers. I was walking on sunshine when I passed because I knew that I would not get fired. I also knew that the tests and the wealth planning process were generic. I was the differentiating factor and now I needed to sell that.

CHAPTER SIXTEEN

Last Day of Training

Matlock and I had met with Weissenstein again to present him some ideas while we were studying for the 7 and 66. Weissenstein gave us some direction on what he would like from us in our final presentation. We were to use a tool that Credit Suisse uses to determine Asset Allocation and Investment Recommendations called Andromeda. This tool allows a Private Banker to enter all of a prospect's portfolio information to do back-testing and forecasting. Then, Andromeda will suggest a model portfolio asset allocation and investments. It will back-test the portfolio vs. the S&P 500 and forecast returns vs. the prospect's current portfolio. The ideal situation is that your suggested portfolio has greater returns than the prospect's current portfolio and less or similar risk.

I used Andromeda to create a diversified portfolio with a theme of China related investments because that's what Weissenstein asked for. I did all the portfolio analysis, and I put all the work into a PowerPoint presentation. Matlock just sat behind me and watched. He didn't contribute a single keystroke. I was a little annoyed that I had to do everything so I decided I would throw Matlock under the bus. The best way to do that was to let him talk out loud in front of people about investments. If he had to do that, then he was doomed. I was also a little sneaky and purposely didn't put any investments in his portion. I gave him a general asset allocation that said we would put 30% in bonds, 50% in equity, 15% in alternative investments, and 5% in cash. I could have put in some information about investments in there, but I thought it would be my last day of training and I wanted to have some fun. I couldn't think of anything more fun than seeing Weissenstein demolish Matlock. For my China portion, I dug around on the Credit Suisse intranet and found a report that

Weissenstein wrote about investing in China. The report offered his own personal recommendations. I used these recommendations and then made sure to know everything about them. I was prepared. Half of our presentation would suck and half would pass. It was the last day and I was fine with that. I was tired and wanted to fly home and see my wife.

All of the Associates would file into a conference room one last time to give one last Weissenstein presentation. It was apparent that we all felt the same way: just give the presentation, it doesn't matter what you say, you will still get hammered on it. When Matlock stood up in front of everyone, he read the bullet points that I wrote on the slides. He compared Weissenstein's portfolio to our new suggested portfolio. And, of course as the Chief Investment Officer, Weissenstein asked, "what are you going to invest in?"

"Ummm. We are going to invest 30% in bonds, 50% in equity and 15% alternative investments." Answered Matlock.

"Yes. I can read. What bonds? What Equity? What Alternative Investments?" Whined Weissenstein.

"Well, we didn't do that, but it's something we can get back to you on."

"That's your job right? You invest in stocks, bonds and alternative investments. You couldn't pick just one investment?"

"Umm. Our next slide has investments on it."

I sat there and loved every single second of it. The next slides were my China slides. I went on to present all of Weissenstein's ideas back to him. I offered him debt, equity and alternative investments that had a China theme to them and gave him exactly what he asked for: a diversified portfolio with a China theme running through it. He fired questions at me.

"What does the China Private Equity Fund Invest in? What is the expense ratio of the Xinhua 25 ETF? How does buying a YUM Brands bond have a China theme?"

I answered all of his questions and when it was time for him to evaluate me all he said was, "China. China. China. All you do is talk about China."

In reality, all Weissenstein does is talk about China. He's been bullish on China for years and makes it his calling card. He can't go through a discussion about investments without discussing China. I spoon-fed him his own ideas and he still didn't have anything nice to say.

After the last presentation was done, Weissenstein cheered up a bit. He admitted that he was overly harsh on us, but it was for our own good. It would make us better in real meetings. He bid us good luck and I would never have to give him another presentation again. He would only live on in research reports, investor conference calls, and CNBC Power Lunch interviews. In our training wrap-up, Eric Dale said that we weren't completely done with him. In exactly nine months, we would be flown back to do one last case called "Final Check" all on our own to be graded by the Private Bank's top executives. If you didn't pass you would have to keep doing it until you did pass.

My closest friend in the US Associate Class, Northwestern-Chicago, and I took the elevator down to Eleven Madison Park for celebratory cocktails. We cheers'd to our new life as Private Bankers and bid each other farewell until "Final Check." It was Friday afternoon and on Monday we would begin working as Private Bankers. We were done with training. We were excited. We were going to make so much money!

PART II:

THE JOB

CHAPTER SEVENTEEN

Time to Shake Your Money Maker

My first day began as most MBA's first day back in the workforce begins. I woke before the sun rose with $137,988 in Student Loans, put on my work clothes (for my first day it was Hugo Boss suit, shoes, belt, tie and a pair of shiny shiny cufflinks from Hermes) and headed to work. I was the first person in the office that morning. The lights turned on as I entered the office space. I didn't know where my desk would be so I found an empty desk next to the manager's office. I plugged in my laptop and listened to the morning research call. By the time the call was over, there was still no one in the office. A few assistants started to trickle in at 8 a.m., but no Private Bankers until about 9 a.m. I worked on polishing my cold call spiel, "Hi, this is W.E. Kidd from Credit Suisse…etc." I read some research and when the manager's assistant arrived, she showed me where my desk would be.

My desk location was the first sign of my place in the office, literally and figuratively. To the right of the manager's office was where everyone sat. It was full of lights and offices and cubicles. To the left of the manager's office was a sea of empty cubicles, about twenty-five in total. In the middle of this sea of cubicles is where my desk would be. I would be sitting next to no one. I could get attacked by the janitor and no one would discover my body for days. It was dead quiet and empty.

"Where's Matlock going to sit?" I asked.

"Oh, he'll sit across from you." Said the office manager's assistant.

Fantastic. Empty cubes to the left of me. Empty cubes to the right. Here I am stuck in the middle with Matlock.

The first thing that hits you as you sit down at your new desk on your first day on the job is that there's no work for you to do and there's no one that's going to tell you to do any work. On any Private Banking job information site, one of the top requirements is for the applicant to be entrepreneurial. This description translates approximately to "ability to work by one's self without anyone giving them any work to do."

There are a couple of ways that people handle the opportunity to make $60,000 signing bonus and $95,000 per year for two years without anyone ever telling them to do anything. The first way to handle this situation is to do nothing, take the money, and basically get paid for doing nothing. And, when I say do nothing I mean you don't even have to come into the office. You stay at home and make money. I know you're thinking that this is impossible, but Matlock did it and he took it to the extreme. This is one of the last times I'll mention Matlock because from this point on he did nothing. Yes, from our first day on he did nothing. According to my calculations he took approximately one hundred and thirteen days off during his first year. There are only two hundred and thirty work days in a year! I think this must be some kind of Credit Suisse record. At first, I felt angry with Matlock because I felt like he was getting away with something. Then, my emotions turned from anger to admiration.

Matlock and the new head of the office never liked each other. While we were finishing our last year of MBA, Lehman Brothers went bankrupt. On that very same day, the head of the Atlanta Lehman Brothers office, Tom Cooper, became head of the Atlanta Credit Suisse office. Cooper replaced Michael Sterling, the man who hired me. Cooper would be the person who paid Jeremy Jones an $11 million signing bonus, but we'll get into that later.

Tom Cooper is a University of Georgia graduate and head of Sigma Nu for the Southeast. He would later brag to his Sigma Nu mentees at a chapter meeting that it took him only three hours to find a new job in the middle of the worst Recession since the Great

Depression. Matlock had interviewed for a summer internship with Cooper at Lehman Brothers and Cooper had basically told him in the interview that he would never be successful as a Private Banker. Matlock described it as his worst interview ever. For some reason, Cooper hated Matlock and refused to speak to him. It was like something out of *Catch-22*. Watching the two of them was like watching Yosssarian and Major Major. Just like Major Major, Cooper would ignore all of Matlock's requests for a meeting and always say he was busy if Matlock came by to talk. After a little of this Matlock probably said to himself, "if I have no one to report to and no one telling me to do anything and Cooper will not talk to me, then I'm probably not going to make it past two years. So, I'll do zero work and see how long I can get away with it. I'll take off over one hundred days. I'll come into the office for an hour and call it a day. I'll sit at my desk and just read the Internet for a year. Cooper will not talk to me and to get fired he will have to talk to me. So, logically I'm safe." For this, I gave Cooper the nickname Major Major Cooper.

Major Major Cooper didn't talk to me on my first day either. However, where Matlock got paid to do nothing, I got paid to try. That's what this part of my story is about. Me trying. Hopefully you'll learn a little about Private Banking and Investing along the way.

The first thing I had to try to do was to get a meeting with a millionaire. As a Private Banker with no clients, this was my only job at the moment. Get a meeting. Bud Fox had it a little easier in the eighties because he could pick up the phonebook and dial anyone. In fact in that first scene in *Wall Street* you see the phonebook open on Bud's desk and he is cold calling people. Like I said earlier, my job was more like the Gekko scene over and over. Call the millionaires. So, I put together a list of millionaires I would call. The only thing Major Major Cooper said to me during my first six months at the firm was, "Show me your list." So, I printed out my list of about five hundred names. We sat in his office as he went through each name. He grunted and crossed off a name every time he came across one that was a client or currently being pursued by someone else in the office. Then, he gave my list back to me.

"It's a start," he said.

I was then left on my own to cold call.

The song "Got Nuffin" by Spoon ran through my head as I made these calls. The line "got nothing to lose but loneliness and hang-ups" perfectly described the act of cold calling for me.

I would bring my list of names with me into a conference room and close the door. I wanted it to be just my list, the phone, and me. No distractions. It was lonely and people would hang-up on me so the Spoon song nailed that feeling. My objective was to get someone to talk to me and to then get them to meet with me. A majority of these calls ended in hang-ups, voice mail or an assistant. Or, as I like to call them "the Natalie's." That was the name of Gekko's assistant that Bud would always talk to. You've got to be nice to the Natalie's because they can really help you get a meeting.

"Hello Natalie. Recognize the voice? Here's a hint. You're thinking about marrying me." Schmoozed Bud.

I only wish I was half that good with "the Natalie's" of the world. Being good with the Natalie's is essential because they are so much more than just a gatekeeper or an assistant, they are your connection to the prospect.

In addition to cold calling, I would do cold emailing. The cold email is a brand new thing that Bud Fox never had in his toolbox, but it is basically the same concept of reaching out to someone you don't know to sell them something they don't want. Instead of having them hang up on you or getting a voice mail, you just never hear from them again. For some reason this form of rejection is much easier to deal with. When I was first starting out, I would tell myself if I had a day when one person returned one phone call or email, then that was a good day. I would go home pretty darn happy with myself. I would send cold emails to people, cold call them and send them research in the regular mail. I would look for common connections to mention, ways to network in and eventually I would get meetings. I bet my meeting conversion rate was about twenty percent. The first big meeting I ever got was through cold calling and cold emailing. I still have the response that the CEO's Natalie had sent me. This Natalie's name was Suzanne.

"Hello W.E.…As we discussed when you called, he is out of the office until mid-December. He did receive the information that you sent and he is interested in setting up a meeting with you after he returns to the office. He is available on December 14, 15, 17 and 18. Since we are so far in advance of that date, you would have a choice as far as what time you would like to meet. Please look at your calendar and let me know what would work best for you and we'll set something up. Thank you, Suzanne."

I wanted to jump out of my chair and high-five someone, but there was no one there to high-five. I sat in the middle of no man's land and worked by myself. So, I did a Tiger Woods fist pump and felt very pleased with myself. I just got my first big meeting.

When the day of the meeting arrived, I got there about twenty minutes early and sat in the parking lot in my car and studied my notes. After my twenty minutes of waiting, I grabbed my pitchbook and a research report that I thought the CEO would enjoy and checked in with reception. I told them I had an appointment with the CEO. They gave me a badge and escorted me up to his office where I met Suzanne and thanked her for all her help. I walked into the CEO's office and introduced myself.

"Hi, nice to meet you. Glad we could find time to meet in person," I said.

I'm pretty good at reading facial expressions and I couldn't help but notice that there was a somewhat terrified expression on the CEO's face. It immediately hit me. The CEO was seventy-one. I was thirty-three, but I could have passed for twenty-three. I've got a young face, which isn't exactly a bonus in the business world. He was looking at me as if to say, "I can't believe I just took a meeting with a teenager." There's nothing I could do about it other than show him I had a brain and try to make a connection. I told him that we might have a friend in common. I dropped the friend's name and he said, "Of course, he was one of the founders of the company." It was a good icebreaker and after we chatted about how I knew one of the founders, I went into my pitch. I had been working on my pitch for months. I felt like all of my training led up to that moment. All of my Weissenstein presentations and practice calls and product pitches and research had prepared me and I proceeded to give what was in my opinion the best, most polished pitch I would ever give for the bank. Everything was so fresh in my mind and I had been doing nothing but practicing up to that point so my presentation was perfect. I covered how Credit Suisse was founded and why we were different, our presence in the United States, the firm's work in the CEO's industry, how we developed relationships with clients, what we had been doing for clients, our thoughts on the economy, how we structured portfolios, some investment themes we were currently using in portfolios, how those themes reflected what we had been seeing in the markets and our forecasts for the next year. I was pitch perfect.

After giving the greatest speech of my entire life, the CEO just stared at me and didn't utter a word. So, I asked what he had been doing. "How have you been managing your portfolio?" I asked. It was a nice open-ended question. I was textbook baby. His response was, "I've been using the same financial advisor for over twenty years. Do you have any materials you can leave behind?"

"Of course," I said. "I've made this pitchbook that will elaborate on all the different solutions that we offer in Private Banking and I thought you might enjoy this research."

"Thanks for stopping by," he said as he shooed me out.

The whole time he was looking at me like I was far too young to even consider talking to. Natalie/Suzanne escorted me back to the lobby. I handed in my badge. The company is publicly traded on the New York Stock Exchange under the ticker CRY. After that awful first meeting that was all I wanted to do: CRY.

CHAPTER EIGHTEEN

Where Have All The Stockbrokers Gone? Part II

David Maude, a former McKinsey & Company consultant turned author literally wrote the book on Private Banking and Wealth Management. In his textbook *Global Private Banking and Wealth Management* published in 2006 by Wiley Finance, Maude did some research that I love. He did a Factiva search on the number of English language-only press articles using the term "Wealth Management" and then did the same search for the term "Private Banking." He graphed the massive rise in the number of articles about the subject from 1996 to 2005. I think his work shows that after E-trade went public, the terms Private Banking and Wealth Management took off. I think it shows the death of the stockbroker and the rise of Private Banking and Private Wealth Management. Maude's graph is below.

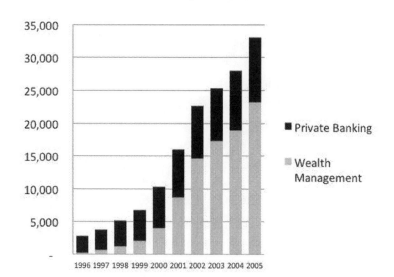

David Maude's Factiva Search

Here is my graph doing the exact same Factiva search as David Maude, but bringing the numbers up to 2010:

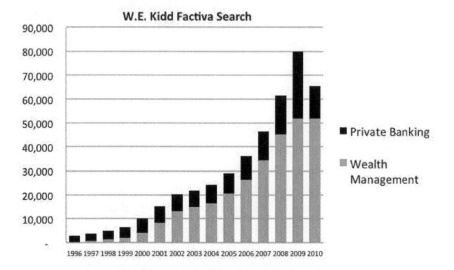

I think Maude's research is interesting and proves his point that Private Banking and Wealth Management have risen out of practically nothing back in the mid-nineties. He named his graph "the rise and rise of wealth management." When I updated Maude's numbers, I was hoping for an increase, but I wasn't expecting the massive increase I found. My numbers aren't an exact match to Maude's because Factiva will add in new publications and update its algorithm, but the numbers are close enough that I felt confident I performed the same steps as Maude. I discovered that in the five years since Maude did his search, Private Banking has more than tripled and Wealth Management has more than doubled. Can somebody please create a financial product that mimics the number of press articles that include Private Banking and Wealth Management? I want to invest in that. Imagine a graph of the Dow Jones Industrial Average up there. From 2000 to 2009 you would see it decrease from 10,000 to 8,000 while Private Banking/Wealth Management rose from 10,000 to

80,000. Call your stockbroker and see if they can create this product for you. Oh, wait, stockbrokers are dead.

After I recreated Maude's research and updated it, I went ahead and did a search of my own on the term "stockbroker" to see if I was right in saying that the stockbroker is dead. Here's what I found:

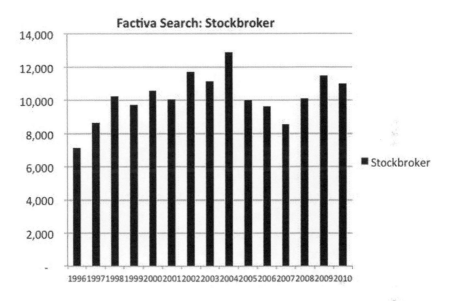

Stockbrokers peaked in 2004 and have actually been relatively flat since 1998. I didn't expect it to be zero or anything. The word stockbroker is still out there, but it's not hot. It's not a buzz word. It's old and not growing.

I thought that replicating and updating David Maude's data and doing a similar search for the term stockbroker proved my point that Private Banking and Wealth Management had overtaken stockbrokers, but I wasn't satisfied with just recreating Maude's search. I wanted to improve upon it and make it my own. Maude's search was very simple. All he did was type the terms into Factiva's search engine and press the "run" button. It doesn't get any easier than that. It's how most people search these days. You type something into Google and then you press the search button. Easy. However, there are more refined ways of searching and I wanted to one-up Maude and take this thing to the next level. I knew I didn't have the skills to do it on my own, so I enlisted some help. I contacted my favorite business librarian at Emory University, Susan Klopper, and she schooled me in the art of search.

We met in her office and I explained Maude's search. She then asked me, "Are you comfortable with Bolean logic?"

I vaguely recalled seeing the name in a math textbook. Then, she began typing a search that looked like an Excel formula.

"Oh. You mean like an Excel formula. Yeah. We're good to go." I said.

As she was typing, she would only use root words and then type an asterisk at the end. This type of searching is called Unlimited Truncation and captures any variations that occur from the symbol onward. Through our trial and error, I also picked up some Factiva advanced search functionality.

Armed with Bolean logic, Truncation, and Factiva, which is the only database that has access to full *Wall Street Journal* articles because it is owned by News Corp., I built my search.

Here's what my search looked like:

(stock broker* or stockbroker*) and sn=(wall street journal) and wc>800

(private bank*) and sn=(wall street journal) and wc>800

(wealth manage*) and sn=(wall street journal) and wc>800

Take that David Maude.

You're probably wondering what all of that means. I'm sure
you get the truncation part, but the sn and the wc are Factiva
specific functions. By saying sn=(wall street journal), I narrowed
my search to only *The Wall Street Journal*. I did this because *The
Wall Street Journal* is the bible of financial publications and I
wanted to see if my theory held up in *The Wall Street Journal*
alone without including the thousands of other publications in the
Maude search. The wc>800 is a way to return articles longer than
800 words. I did this to eliminate short articles and repetitive wire
stories. I just wanted substantive articles. My results are below:

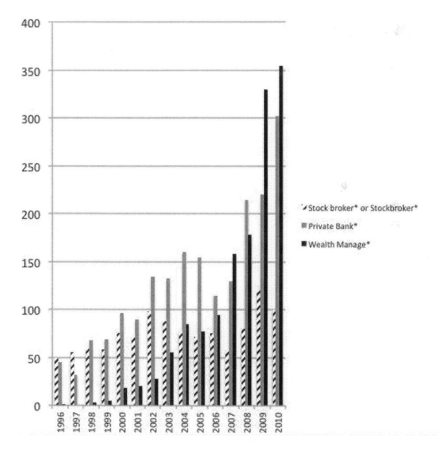

In 1996, the term stock broker* or stockbroker* was used in more articles in *The Wall Street Journal* than either Private Bank* or Wealth Manage*. By 2010, Private Bank* and Wealth Manage* articles would blow away stock broker* or stockbroker*. My search of *The Wall Street Journal* led to similar results as the David Maude search. Since 1996, the year E*Trade went public, Private Banking and Wealth Management have exploded.

There's a very significant historical event caught in the chart above. I began my search with 1996 data. I did it only because that's what Maude did, but 1996 is very significant. Maybe Maude lucked into it or maybe he knew what he was doing. If you look at 1996 on the graph, there is a tiny bump representing Wealth Manage*. In fact, the term Wealth Manage* was only in one article for all of 1996. I thought this was interesting so I searched to see if Wealth Manage* was mentioned prior to 1996. It wasn't. I even took out my word count restriction and still found nothing. 1996 was the first time the term Wealth Management was used in the history of *The Wall Street Journal*. When I discovered this, I felt like a financial Indiana Jones.

In 1996, *The Wall Street Journal* wrote its very first article with the term Wealth Manage* in it. In 2010 there would be 354 articles: more than one per issue. When that happens, it means Wall Street just invented something new. I was curious about who wrote that first article and what it said, so I dug a little further.

The article was titled "Family Offices for Rich Are Booming" and it was written by Laura Jereski on March 6th 1996. Here's how the term is used in the article:

"The boom in wealth management, says Robert Elliott, a senior executive vice president at Bessemer Trust Co., is one of America's least-known growth industries. That growth stems chiefly from the long-booming market for initial public stock offerings, which overnight turns many family-owned enterprise into a pile of cash. This instant wealth confronts newly minted millionaires with a novel dilemma: what to do with their now liquid fortunes."

Robert Elliott of Bessemer Trust called the Wealth Management boom and was the first person ever to utter the term in *The Wall Street Journal*. One of my favorite writers, Wallace Stegner, once wrote that "the tracing of ideas is a guessing game. We can't tell who first had an idea; we can only tell who first had it influentially, who formulated it in a striking way and left it in some form, poem or equation or picture, that others could stumble upon with the shock of recognition." After finding *The Wall Street Journal* article, I had that shock of recognition. Next, I looked up Robert Elliott. The guy still works at Bessemer Trust and had since 1975. He sounded like a leader I could admire.

When I look at all of this data I like to think about where I was when I was deciding to work in Private Banking and how the industry has changed over the years. I like to think about how the terms Private Banking and Wealth Management replacing the term Stockbroker acknowledges the changes in the industry. I look up at the charts and think about my first finance internship in 1997 with Charlie Berry at Bear Stearns Private Client Services. I see that Private Banking and Wealth Management just hadn't taken off in the public's mind at the time. Then, Bear Stearns' Charlie Berry just pitched stocks. Back then I didn't think that being a stockbroker was cool and the persona of Private Wealth Management and Private Banking weren't hot yet. So, I read *Liar's Poker* and went into Asset Securitization. The banks weren't putting their money in Private Banking at the time either. Back then, a new stockbroker with no clients wasn't getting a $60,000 signing bonus and $100,000 salary. That's what it is now because it has become hot. It's not just hot for MBAs that want to get the job. It's also hot for CEOs that are making the decisions to put the jobs and big offers out there. Think about Jeremy Jones. $11 million dollar signing bonus. This was not happening in the mid-nineties.

I look at the year 2007 (the year I first got my summer offer from Credit Suisse) to 2009 (the year I started full-time at Credit Suisse) and can see how popular Private Banking and Wealth Management had become. I think to myself, maybe Credit Suisse bought me at the top? Maybe Credit Suisse was buying high and selling low. When I look at the graphs, I can see why so many people were asking me how to get a Private Banking job: the term was in the press and popular.

I could tell by looking at the charts that the job had become important in the eyes of the press. These charts represent a popularity contest. Private Bankers and Private Wealth Managers are the cool kids. Stockbrokers are not. Private Bankers and Private Wealth Managers are Showtime, HBO and AMC original series. Stockbrokers are the WB. So, why did Private Banking and Private Wealth Management become so hot? Why did I get $60,000 signing bonus and $95,000 salary without any clients to speak of? Why did Jeremy Jones, in the midst of the Great Recession, get $11 million for standing up from his desk on the 6th floor, taking the elevator to the 4th floor, and sitting back down?

If you look at the charts and start to think about the differences between a stockbroker and a Private Banker, you will see why Private Banking signing bonuses sky rocketed at the exact same time that the bonuses on the rest of Wall Street were getting cut. You can see why Private Banking went on a hiring spree while Investment Banking jobs were getting slashed. All you have to do is think about those graphs in terms of revenue. If you follow the money, you find all the answers.

Back in the eighties and nineties the way that people invested their money was to give their broker a commission on each sale. These commissions were much bigger than they are now because there was no other alternative. There was no online broker. A stockbroker would trade stocks and all of these commissions would turn into a good salary. In the late nineties and over the last decade, commissions got slashed. Why pay massive fees when you can go to an online broker?

Wall Street had to reinvent itself. Stockbrokers disappeared. Private Bankers were the new new thing. And, even though they were the new new thing, they were being governed by rules that were established in the 1940 Investment Advisors act. Brokers and clients never fully embraced fee-based accounts until E-Trade started offering $7 trades. Instead of paying a commission, now you would pay an annual fee–typically 1–2% of your assets. Stockbrokers found a way to keep making the 1-2% they were accustomed to, but now they could do it without even having to place a lot of trades.

The marketing for Private Banking fee-based accounts was really smart. Banks would say to clients, "Back in the eighties and nineties stockbrokers would churn clients and do a lot of useless trading to increase their revenue. Well, we don't do that anymore. We charge you a 1-2% fee on total assets so that we are incentivized to grow your assets and not churn your account."

Investors said to themselves, "Wow, our incentives are finally aligned and they shelled over the 1%." However, the fee only works on certain types of accounts: big ones. One percent on a $10 million dollar account works for a Private Banker. One percent on a $100,000 account doesn't work for a Private Banker. The $10 million account pays $100,000 in fees and the $100,000 account pays $1,000 in fees. The $10 million account has to pay $99,000 more per year for the same work just because they are richer. You would think this math was invented by a bunch of Democrats. You're richer, you pay more. Essentially, that is Private Banking. In order to go after these big massive accounts, brokers from the nineties formed teams during the last decade. One person on the team would go after family offices, another would go after pension funds, and another would go after business owners getting million-dollar payouts for selling their business. Then, they would hire a twenty-something year old kid just out of undergrad to manage the accounts and answer the phones.

Private Bankers didn't trade the accounts anymore like Stockbrokers did. Most Private Bankers opened the account and then placed the money with different asset managers and said "this is how Yale does it." This was the invention of Private Banking in its latest form. And, because Private Bankers were now only going after these massive accounts that bring in massive fees, they were paid massive amounts of money. Part of the reason behind why they got paid more is because they were now making steady revenue for the firm. No more relying on hot stock tips and churning accounts which is what stockbrokers did. A stockbroker could crush it one year and then make some bad picks the next year and his income would get demolished. Most Private Bankers give assets to other asset managers and charge an annual fee. Every year you know exactly how much you are going to make: x% of assets under management. Private Bankers became a massive source of steady cash flow for a firm. Investment Banking revenue and Sales & Trading Revenue could be inconsistent for firms. Those groups could be up one year and down the next. Or worse, Investment Banking and Sales & Trading could lose money for a bank! Private Banking revenues became the bond in the portfolio: firms knew the Private Banking division would now produce steady cash flows year to year. And, where the money flows is where the talent and interest flows. Banks started to PAY for Private Bankers. The money being generated for Private Bankers was drawing a lot of attention. It became popular. It became cool. And, I think that's what Maude's chart shows. I think my chart just shows that stockbrokers are dead. You could pay someone like Jeremy Jones $11 million because if he brought over all his clients, you knew about how much he would generate per year for the rest of his career. However, if he was just a stockbroker, there was no guarantee of revenues because revenues were only based on number of and size of trades and that could vary widely. Banks don't like volatile revenues. They like to be able to forecast revenues for years and years to come and that's what fee based Private Banking accounts enabled banks to do.

David Maude's chart really got me thinking about the evolution of Private Banking over the past ten years and I thought that I could see the result of that evolution sitting right in front of me in the form of Jeremy Jones in his jeans and millions. Someone had to profit from the new game that Wall Street created and he played it better than most. I will leave you one last thing I love about David Maude. If you buy his book, you will notice that just below the "Rise and Rise of Wealth Management" chart he wrote the following:

David Maude
Verona, May 2006
david_maude@lycos.co.uk

Bolding his name was a nice touch. I think it's amazing that he gave his email. It's even more amazing that it's Lycos. Lycos? Gmail was launched in 2004 buddy.

CHAPTER NINETEEN

Marvel Team-Up

Marvel Team-Up is a series of comics that will typically feature two Marvel characters in one story–usually Spiderman plus someone else. The original series began in 1972 and since then a new writer will pick it up every once in a while. For instance, Robert Kirkman of AMC's *Walking Dead* fame did an eleven issue series in 2005. As seen in the past, Kirkman used Spiderman as the main team-up character. The point to the series is that sometimes you can't go it alone, you need to team-up with someone to win. One of the most popular *Marvel Team-Up's* is Spiderman and Wolverine, two loners that band together for an issue to fight the good fight.

After getting nowhere on my own in my meeting with the CEO of Cryolife, it became apparent to me that I was going to need to do a Marvel Team-Up. However, deciding whom to team-up with is not an easy decision. You need to make sure that your skills are aligned and that your personalities mesh. A lot of people will team-up because they cover different types of clients. One might be good at bringing in foundations and the other might be good at working with executives of public companies. For me, I needed to find someone in the office that could be a mentor and would be someone I would feel comfortable introducing to people in my network. Shortly after my meeting with the CEO of Cryolife, I met a prospect in the elevator of our building who was interested in a particular Hedge Fund we offered to clients. The prospect and I had set a time to meet in our office and I was not going into this meeting solo. I was going to find my Marvel Team-Up and win the business.

Being the newest person in the office, I would always make sure that I was first in and last out. Most Private Bankers will leave when the market closes at 4 p.m. However, I would work until about 7 p.m. and then do a walk around the office to make sure that I was the last one there. I was determined to be the last. When 7 p.m. rolled around, there would only be two people in the office. Alex Finn, the second oldest guy in the office and in his sixties, and me. The oldest guy, Steve Blackburn, was his partner and in his seventies. They were just two old guys that worked by themselves. They weren't a team that I rotated on during my Summer Associate internship so I never got to know them. As I was trying to be the last one in the office at night, old Elliot Finn was giving me some competition. So, I got to know the competition.

It was about 7 p.m. and as usual, Alex and I were the only ones left in the office. I was a little intimidated because Alex never spoke to anyone and didn't want any new Associates rotating on his team the previous summer. In my mind, he was probably some grumpy old man that didn't want to deal with young new Associates like me that he had seen come and go throughout the years. I walked up to his office and gave one of those quiet little knocks on the door that I think only occur on office doors. The quiet knock that you can only hear if you are sitting at your desk ten feet away. I walked in, introduced myself and noticed that his office had a mad scientist feel to it. There were stacks of folders and papers everywhere. He operated completely different than everyone else in the office. Research was spread out everywhere, his desk was a mess and he stayed late when every other Private Banker had left hours before him leaving behind clean desks and assistants to run the show. This was the type of stuff that investors and clients never got to see and it wasn't something that you could put in a pitchbook. You couldn't put research crazy guy that is always at his desk and works weekends on a PowerPoint slide. It just wouldn't work. You have to see it for yourself to buy into it. My immediate impression was that Alex Finn was different, maybe a little crazy, but I liked it. He wasn't a grumpy old man at all. He was like a nice soft-spoken grandpa.

I learned a lot about Alex that night. We both grew up in Chicago, both went to Emory, and both believed in doing right by investors. The doing right by investors thing is something that maybe everyone has the intention of doing, but maybe not everyone does . That night I learned the Alex Finn style. It involved keeping costs low, investing simple and only helping those that need help. When I asked him a little about how he invested he said, "Well, it depends on what the investor wants the portfolio to do." So, I thought I would start with the ultimate simple question.

"How do you build bond portfolios?" I asked.

"I'll use our municipal or corporate bond desk. I'll charge a dollar a bond. For a bond portfolio, it doesn't make sense to charge a management fee. I'll just charge a dollar a bond. It's the minimum that the desk lets me charge. Right now we are laddering maturities and keeping duration very short term because we think interest rates will go up. Since round lots of bonds are sold in increments of 100 at $1,000 par value, I'll charge $100 on $100,000 of bonds."

For those of you non-finance people, this is ten basis points. It's cheap.

"Here, let me show you a portfolio of international bonds I put together last year for a client. See, I used Australian, Swedish, Norwegian and French bonds. Here is how much the bonds have appreciated in price over the past year. 28%. Plus, they earned about 6% interest."

Alex basically just showed me that his bond portfolio blew away stocks in 2009. His bonds crushed the stock market returns.

Then, I asked the next most logical question. "How do you build equity portfolios?"

Alex referred to this as "gentleman's risk." I thought that made it sound so dignified: like smoking jackets and scotch. Gentleman's risk. "For an all equity portfolio, I'll use ETFs and individual stocks. I use ETFs for two purposes. First, to diversify across regions and asset classes. US Large Cap, US Mid-Cap, US Small Cap, Foreign Developed, Foreign Emerging and perhaps commodities. I'll also use ETFs to drill down on certain themes, sectors or countries that the firm looks favorably upon. For instance, I'll use the ETF SMH to drill down on semiconductors. If I really want to get granular, I'll use individual stocks. I'll also just build stock portfolios if investors want say a high dividend yielding stock portfolio. I'll typically make quarterly adjustments and will make adjustments intra quarter if Steve and I see the need to move quickly."

"So, you manage it yourself using all of the research within Credit Suisse?" I asked.

"Yes. Mostly. It's cheaper for the investor that way. I'll charge 1% or lower. If I placed money with an outside manager or mutual fund, then the fees would be higher." He was conscious of the fees. "I don't go around selling low fees, it's just something that I believe in," he said. "I also believe in getting paid for the work that I do."

"Do you use any outside managers?" I asked.

"Sure. If there is a part of the market that I can't get access to or don't have expertise in then I'll use an outside manager. Say for instance Convertible Bonds or South Africa. If I wanted to make a strategic move in a portfolio using convertible bonds, I might consider an outside manager. And, if there wasn't a good ETF alternative to access a foreign market like South Africa, then I might consider an outside manager. Otherwise, I make the trades. The same goes for hedge funds and private equity. With those investments, you have to give the assets to a fund manager."

It made perfect sense to me. A buck a bond. 1% or lower for a portfolio you build using the firm's research analysts, economists and your own brain; only use expensive fund managers to access parts of the market you couldn't access without them.

I liked Alex and thought he was perfect for a Marvel Team-Up. I told him about the prospect meeting that I had set up and that the prospect was interested in a certain hedge fund called the Seer TALF. If you recall, Tim Geitner and the US Government chose nine firms to partner with on its TALF: Term Asset Loan Facility. The TALF funds were to initially focus on commercial mortgage-backed securities and nonagency mortgage backed securities issued before 2009. These were "toxic" assets that Seer would buy at a very low discount from the government and manage on behalf of investors. Having a background in securitization, I thought the investment was compelling. Alex said that he recently bought some SEER TALF for a client, but we should just go into the meeting together with an open mind and see what the prospect had been doing with his portfolio in addition to discussing Seer. I was excited. Now, I had an expert on my side.

On the day of the meeting, I reserved us the largest conference room in the office. The prospect arrived on time and all of us sat down at one end of a long rectangular conference table. I introduced the prospect to Alex and we made some small talk until Alex kicked off the meeting by asking the prospect, "What have you been doing?" It was an open-ended question and it worked. The investor said that he had been trying to maintain a diversified portfolio and was looking for a way to access the distressed real estate market either through a distressed real estate fund manager or through personally buying distressed real estate himself. He said that purchasing distressed TALF or PPIP assets was an investment he would like to consider. The prospect told us the size of his portfolio and that he had recently come into some money that he would like to put to work. He said that through the downturn, he had remained invested in equities and never sold in a panic.

However, given the specifics of his portfolio and his general demeanor, both Alex and I could tell that the TALF and PPIP probably weren't what the investor was looking for.

Alex turned the conversation over to me to describe the investments. After my description, it became obvious that the Seer TALF was closing too soon and its minimum investment was too high. And, the Marathon PPIP's 8-year lock-up was a lot longer than the prospect wanted to have his money in an illiquid investment. I could see a sense of relief on the prospect's face because we weren't going to give him the hard sell. Once we learned a little more about him, it was obvious that the investments weren't appropriate for him. All of us realized that. When Alex acknowledged that and took the meeting in a new direction, the prospect really responded. Alex took over the meeting and described how we manage portfolios using ETFs and individual bonds. He described what he had been doing for clients and his thoughts for the upcoming year. We went off on a few tangents – muni bonds, international bonds, college savings. Alex ended the conversation saying that we could perform an analysis of the prospect's portfolio and give him our thoughts and ideas. The prospect loved it. Alex brought me back into the meeting by saying that the prospect should give his account statements to me and that I would be the point of contact and the one using our internal software to perform the analysis. We also set a time to meet again in a week to discuss our analysis. It was brilliant. I got the statements the next day.

I spent a week analyzing the portfolio. I back-tested it, I stress tested it, and I compared it to our Weissenstein recommended allocations. I calculated annualized returns over the past three years and volatility. One of the funniest quirks of using Credit Suisse's internal software was that it would provide annualized returns for the past three years, which in 2009 were negative numbers. So, I was basically comparing the prospects negative return over the past three years to Weissenstein's suggestions which had a slightly less negative return over the past three years. It was like saying, "Pay us and we will lose less." Not a compelling argument.

After a week of making sure I modeled the portfolio perfectly, I went into Alex's office and showed him my analysis. He looked at all the work I did and said, "Well…it looks like he's doing a pretty good job managing it himself. I don't think there is much we can do. He should look at adding some more Emerging Markets, but that's it." The funny thing is that I completely agreed. I didn't want to. After training, I figured that if someone gave you their account statements, then the account was as good as yours because we are one of the best private banks in the world and we are brilliant, etc. However, the prospect's portfolio was almost identical to Weissenstein's recommendations.

When we met with the prospect again, we were in the same conference room around the same conference table. We told him that our conclusion was that he was doing a good job on his own and that our only recommendation would be to add more exposure to the emerging markets. The prospect admitted that investing was a hobby for him. He said that he spent a lot of time on it and emerging markets were something he had been considering adding. I presented him with the analysis that I did and he loved it. He had never seen all of his accounts working together on the same page. Since investing was his hobby, he particularly enjoyed receiving back-testing, stress testing and forecasting. He praised my analysis. We told him that unless he got to a point in his life that he was too busy to manage the portfolio so closely, then he should continue managing it himself. He appreciated the honesty. I didn't get my first account that day, but because we were honest, the prospect did give us an introduction to someone he knew who had just won $100 million in the lottery.

During training I would dream of referrals like the $100 million lottery winner. I thought I just hit the jackpot. I thought that this was a guarantee. I was definitely going to open an account and it was going to be massive. I was going to be the person in my Associate class to get unbelievably lucky. Unfortunately, the lottery winner decided to work with the local branch of Edward Jones. We got a conference call with the lottery winner's lawyer but never an in-person meeting. We didn't have an office in the lottery winner's state and that was a deal breaker. The biggest Swiss Private Bank in the world and we lost to a retail brokerage. I would still keep in touch with the first prospect. We had at least developed a friendly relationship. And, I would never give up trying to work for the lottery winner. Neither ever came to fruition. It felt like my first jump at Zur Oepfulchammer: looked like it would be easy at first and ended up being a right challenge. The good that came out of going after the first prospect with Alex was that we both decided that we liked working together. He told me that he would continue to work on prospects with me if I wanted, and of course I did. I wanted to work with someone who was not a salesman, but an investor. In my mind, he was the best in the office. We did the right thing in the meeting even if we didn't open an account.

Emerging Markets happened to perform well in 2010. The EEM was up 12.07% and the VWO was up 14.45%. I was proud of the advice. We were a Marvel Team-Up fighting the good fight.

CHAPTER TWENTY

Discretionary Managed Account

There are three ways to manage money. The first and most simple way is to do it yourself. Open up an online brokerage account, log yourself in, build your own portfolio and make your own trades. The second way is to give it to someone and have them manage it. Imagine giving your money to a Private Banker that makes all the trades in your account for you or to a mutual fund manager. The mutual fund manager doesn't consult you on trades, they do it at their own discretion. The third way to do it is to give the money to someone and then have them give it to someone else to manage. This is like giving your money to your Private Banker (he takes a fee) and then your Private Banker gives the money to a mutual fund manager (he takes a fee) who will then make all the trades.

I know you are thinking that this could go on forever, people just passing money around to one another, taking a fee, but not taking any responsibility to actually do any trading. Industry standard has pretty much decided that you give it to your Private Banker then he gives it to someone else to actually do the investing. There's no more of that stockbroker calling you up and pitching a stock trade anymore. And, for some reason any more parties involved in taking fees and not doing any trading would just seem ridiculous. That is unless you count something that is called a fund of funds. In this case, you give your money to a Private Banker (he takes a fee), he gives your money to a fund of funds manager (he takes a fee),and he gives the money to individual hedge funds (they take a fee) who do the actual investing.

In my mind, the more people involved that don't do anything and just take fees means the more people you don't trust. If you don't trust yourself, then you get a Private Banker. If you don't trust your Private Banker to make the trades, then you tell him to give the money to fund managers.

When I first accepted my offer and told my friends that I was going to be an Associate in Credit Suisse's Private Banking division, most everyone would reply, "Okay. But what do you do?"

I would say, "I'm going to manage investments for high net worth individuals and families."

Everyone would then respond, "You're actually the one that will make all the investments!"

This was typically said with a look saying that there's no way anyone will trust you to do that all by yourself because you have no experience. It's at this point that the conversation would break down because I would have to say that sometimes the Private Banker is the one that makes the investments, but sometimes the Private Banker isn't the one that makes the investments. It just depends.

The type of account where I would be the one making all of the investments is called a Discretionary Managed Account. The discretionary part of the title means that the Private Banker makes all the decisions about the account and makes all the trades. The client pays the Private Banker a fee and that fee is the only money that the Private Banker makes off of the client. The Private Banker will use stocks, bonds, and ETFs, etc. to build the portfolio and make all the trades themselves. Here's an example of what a discretionary portfolio might look like on the following page.

DOMESTIC - 80%			INTERNATIONAL - 20%	
Domestic Large Cap (75%)			International Developed (70%)	
Broad			EFA	45%
SPY	35%		VEA	25%
IVW	20%		EPP	10%
VYM	20%		EWG	5%
			SCZ	5%
Subsector			EWJ	5%
XLP	5%		EWA	5%
IGV	5%		TOTAL	100%
IHE	5%			
IHI	5%			
XLK	5%		International Emerging (30%)	
TOTAL	100%		EEM	47%
			VWO	47%
Domestic Mid Cap (15%)			EWZ	3%
IWR	50%		GMF	3%
IJK	50%		TOTAL	100%
TOTAL	100%			
Domestic Small Cap (10%)				
IWM	50%			
IJT	50%			
TOTAL	100%			

This is the most simple way to have a relationship with a Private Banker because it involves the least amount of parties. It is also cheaper for that same reason. Your Private Banker really knows your account in this case because they are the ones that have made every single trade. This is the way that Alex Finn works. And, it is the way that made the most sense to me and how I wanted to work with my clients. Keep it cheap and take responsibility for the trades.

It takes a special type of Private Banker to manage discretionary portfolios. I would describe this person as smart and blessed with the ability to make money. I honestly think that there is some sort of a gene that some people have and some people don't have and I call it the ability to make money gene. If you have found that you don't possess the ability to buy things and sell them for a profit, then you should not manage discretionary portfolios. You also have to be smart. You have to surround yourself in research, form opinions and execute on an investment strategy. Private Bankers that do not manage discretionary portfolios will say that they don't do it because it is not scalable. They will say,

"How can I manage all these portfolios and still find time to schmooze millionaires on the golf course or while fishing or other schmoozing activities? I don't have the time to make all the trades. I can't be in the office all the time."

All I can say is that these people are at home on the weekends and late nights when Alex is in the office surrounded by his stacks of research, forming opinions and managing all of his accounts. If it sounds like I am biased toward this way of managing clients, it is because I am. In the world of geeks that can schmooze, I lean more toward the geek side of things. And, when you are a geek, you tend to prefer to do your research and make all the trades for a client. Schmoozers prefer to give all their clients' money to someone else to make the trades so they have more time schmoozing on the golf course. All Private Bankers have to be a little bit of both no matter how they manage money. You've got to be a little geek and a little schmooze. It's what makes a Private Banker a Private Banker.

During my time at Credit Suisse, I came to admire another Private Banker that was a geek who preferred to manage assets himself just like Alex and me. His name is Bruce Lee and he works out of the Chicago office. During training, Bruce Lee was constantly referred to as one of the best in the business and rightfully so, he always makes the Barron's Top 100 Financial Advisors in the country. The way that Bruce was described in training made him seem like a bad boy. Associates would say that when he walked into the Chicago office of Credit Suisse, everyone stared in awe because he is not only one of the biggest Private Bankers at Credit Suisse, he is one of the biggest Private Bankers in the country. Eric Dale described him as someone that would curse and slam the phone and his clients would not leave him. Before speaking with Bruce I was expecting him to be much more of a schmoozer than a geek, but I was wrong.

Bruce Lee is 100% geek. He began his career in 1985 and told me that back then you didn't need to be smart to be a stockbroker. Guys that knew nothing about investing could make it. Back then, all that mattered was schmooze and a true salesman could do the job. He told me that now you needed to be intelligent and knowledgeable about portfolio management. When he said that, I asked, "You need to be a geek that can schmooze?"

"Well." He thought about it for a minute. I could tell that he was the type of guy that didn't just agree with someone for the sake of agreeing with them. Then, he said, "Yes."

Since Bruce is one of the biggest Private Bankers in the country, managing over $1 billion, he could have easily jumped to another firm for a bonus even bigger than Jeremy Jones's bonus, but he never did. That's a quality I ascribe to the good ones. I also put him in my category of being one of the good ones because when I asked him how he manages money, he said that he likes to do it himself on a discretionary basis. He said, "I run Discretionary Portfolios and I'll use some Alternative Investments to increase returns. Sometimes, I'll use outside managers, but I've found that I do a better job making the trades myself." That was the exact same reason why I teamed-up with Alex Finn. I thought to myself that Bruce Lee and I could make a good team. Green Hornet and Kato. However, Bruce Lee works alone. No team-ups for him. He's like the Punisher.

CHAPTER TWENTY-ONE

Yes Means Maybe

The first person to tell me that they would open an account with me was someone that I knew. I had been trying many different prospecting strategies. I had put together a list of all Swiss companies with a presence in the southeast and marketed the firm and myself to the executives. I focused on industries that I was familiar with and built out my relationships with those executives. I networked with lawyers and accountants and non-profit organizations. I asked friends for introductions. After all of my work, the first person to say, "Yes I will open an account with you," was someone that I knew before I ever took the Private Banking job.

He was a Jamaican businessman that I had known for about twelve years. We had made plans to meet at Restaurant Eugene to have drinks. I sat at the bar waiting for him with my notebook and PowerPoint slides. He typically would show up for our drinks meetings late, slam a couple of scotches and leave in a rush. He's one of the busiest men I've ever met in my entire life and whenever he says he has time to meet I don't mind sitting by myself at the bar and waiting for him to arrive. This instance was no different. He arrived late and ordered a scotch. Not once has he ever not done this.

"So," he said, "Ow much do you need?"

I smiled and said, "They want us to bring in $40 million over two years. My minimum account size is $500,000." We were close enough that this was something I could share with him.

"Okay…Okay…I see." He thought for a moment. "I'll geev you $500,000 to staht. If you do a good job the first year I'll geev you a million." He paused for a moment and looked me right in the eye. "But I don't want to talk to anybody but you. Credit Suisse. Goldman Sachs. Dees bahnk. Daht bahnk. I don't care. All I care about is you. I'm not in need of a new bahnk. All I care about is you."

"Okay," I replied. It sounded like I just got my first client and I didn't want to mess it up.

"Next time I see you I'll give you a check."

"What do you want the money to do?" I asked.

"I want growth and protection," he said. "I'll be in the Lower Antilles for a couple of weeks and then we can meet again." He finished his scotch and left.

I was elated. I was only a couple of months into the job and I had my first client. It was the exact opposite of my meeting at Cryolife. I was "on" at Cryolife and it got me nowhere because the CEO didn't know me. In this instance, I barely had to utter a word. He said he would open an account with me only because he knew me. Unfortunately, I was soon to find out that when it comes to opening up Private Banking accounts, yes means maybe. There's a massive difference between someone that says, "Yes, I would like to open a Private Banking Account with you," and someone that gives you money. I think the difference is need.

Here's what happened. Our next meeting was at the prospect's office. This time I wasn't going in alone. I was bringing Alex with me. I had a feeling the prospect was going to grill me about investments and I wanted to make sure I had an expert with me and also wanted to show the prospect that I was part of a team: not just me sitting in a cube by myself. Alex and I arrived at the prospect's office and it was very similar to Cryolife. We got our badges, signed in, and then the Natalie took us up to the office. This was the first time I had actually been in the Jamaican's office and got an inside look into his personality. The office was full of huge black and white cricket photographs and equations. It was fitting.

The Jamaican arrived a little later and I introduced him to Alex. I had brought a page of talking points that I wanted to discuss and an account information gathering sheet. Before opening an account, you need to collect info on the client, get a copy of driver's license and put together new account forms. It's nowhere near as easy as just getting a check. There are a ton of forms. So, I had organized the meeting to collect new account information and find out more about what the Jamaican wanted. In our last meeting he said "growth and protection," which I thought was a little vague. I thought having Alex with me to talk to the Jamaican would help me get a sense of how we would invest.

I started by asking the Jamaican, "You said that you want growth and protection, but if you could describe the rest of your portfolio to us or give us statements, then it would help us to compliment your portfolio."

"Look. I'm doing this for him," he said to Alex. "I don't need another bahnk. I just want the money to beat inflation." He turned to me. "What would you do to beat inflation?"

A couple of things occurred to me at that moment. Everyone that I'm going to prospect will most likely already have Private Bankers and have been investing for many years. They are going to bring all of those experiences in the room with them. The good and the bad. Unfortunately, it sounded like the Jamaican had a bad experience with a Private Banker. He didn't even want to talk to Alex. He just wanted to talk to me and wanted me to answer how I would beat inflation. If someone is asking you to beat inflation, they have lost money investing and are not happy about it. That's my only explanation.

It was an odd meeting and I felt like the Jamaican was just placating me and didn't take me seriously. I answered his question by saying that we could invest in treasury inflation protection securities if he wanted to beat inflation. It was a textbook kind of answer and not the right one. He turned to Alex and said, "What do you think?"

Alex in his quiet and wise way said, "Well it sounds to me like you are concerned with another correction in the market, but don't want to be left out if the market is truly in recovery mode. If you want growth and protection I would build a portfolio of half equities and half bonds. I would keep the maturities on the bonds short term with an eye on rising interest rates. I would keep the equities positioned with a view that we will have slow economic growth in developed countries and continued strong growth in emerging countries. And, I would look at "growth" companies because of where we are in the business cycle."

"Okay…what's next."

Alex saved me. We then went through the new account information sheet and said that we would bring the docs for signature and investment ideas for him next week. The meeting didn't last long because the Jamaican never has time to talk. I got my first new account forms filled out. For that I was thankful. However, I couldn't help leaving with a sense that the Jamaican didn't need to open an account and therefore wasn't very cooperative with us or open about how he had been investing.

When I got back to the office I proudly gave the new account information sheets to Alex's assistant to help me put together all of the documentation for signature and then worked with Alex on structuring portfolio recommendations for our signing meeting. Unfortunately, that signing meeting never happened. I never heard from the Jamaican again. He didn't return phone calls or emails. Maybe he had a bad experience with a Private Banker in the past and didn't want to go down the same road again. Maybe he had to take the money and use it for something else. I would never find out. It made me realize that in Private Banking yes means maybe. It also made me realize that I wanted to work for people that actually needed me. Otherwise, I felt like I was going to run into a lot more client relationships like the Jamaican. People that don't have a need will never be good clients or for that matter clients at all.

I later discussed my almost first client with Eric Dale and his advice was, "Why go after smaller $1 million accounts? Go after $50 million accounts and have them give you a small piece." $1 million used to mean something, but not anymore. $1 million was what Gekko gave Bud. The eighties are long gone and no one cares about a million dollars anymore. Stockbrokers left with the eighties.

Bud Fox isn't even a stockbroker anymore. In *Wall Street II*, Bud Fox made an appearance and said that he got out of jail and still became the CEO of the airline and then sold it. I pretended I didn't hear that part of the movie. Bud will always be a stockbroker to me.

The eighties, when $1 million meant something, are over. Bud Fox is a philanthropist. Michael Lewis books are getting turned into Sandra Bullock movies. Bad boy Jay McInerny is now a wine snob for *The Wall Street Journal*. The eighties are gone and a million is nothing. That was the message that I was getting, but I didn't care. To me a million was a lot. If someone wanted to open a million dollar account with Alex and me, we would have worked our tails off for them. Call us old fashioned, but we still thought a million was good money. Now, I just needed to find someone with a million that actually needed help.

Chapter Twenty-Two

Jeremy Jones

Not long after my meeting with the Jamaican, people in the office started whispering about Jeremy Jones. Private Bankers that are not on the same team rarely ever speak to one another, but around February 2010, a lot of teams started whispering to one another.

"Jeremy Jones is coming over."

"Biggest Goldman Sachs team in the southeast."

"$11 million."

"Don't talk to the press."

In 1997 Jon Corzine, then CEO of Goldman Sachs, opened a brand new Goldman Sachs office in Atlanta. The office was a branch of the firm's Private Client Services division. It was the first new U.S. office opened by Goldman Sachs since 1978. At the time, Corzine said that, "Atlanta has always been a vital area for Goldman Sachs because of its geographic importance as the hub of the South and a gateway for international commerce. We have a long history of relationships in Atlanta. Opening an office here brings us that much closer to our partners and clients and allows us to provide even more personalized service."

The office would be located at 3414 Peachtree Road. The exact same building that I would be in thirteen years later when Jeremy Jones sat down right in front of me on the 4th floor $11 million richer than he had been on the sixth floor. Corzine hired a man named Bert Rayle to be office manager and staffed the office with twenty-two additional new hires to, as the announcement said, "provide personal investment counseling." One of those new hires in 1997 was Jeremy Jones. At the time all of this was taking place, I was in the same building complex working for Charlie Barry at

Bear Stearns. At that time if you would have told me that my life would lead me to working with Jeremy Jones thirteen years later in the same building I wouldn't have believed you because Private Banking wasn't hot at the time. I'm sure that if you told Jeremy Jones in 1997 that in 2010 the market would be in the exact same place, but that he would be getting $11 million to move two floors he would have said you were crazy. Yet, here we were. The market hadn't moved in thirteen years and Jeremy Jones was a millionaire sitting right in front of me. Sitting in my cube with my zero clients, I couldn't help but wonder how this happened and how Jeremy Jones manages money.

In 1997, Jeremy Jones was an accountant at Arthur Anderson working for corporate executives. Luckily for him, he left the company before the Enron scandal and was recruited by Goldman to join what was then called Goldman Sachs Private Client Services. His title would be Investment Advisor. Now they call it Private Wealth Management. The point is that before being a hot shot Private Banker making millions, Jeremy Jones was a boring old accountant at a now defunct accounting firm.

Goldman had just made the perfect hire because Jeremy Jones wasn't some MBA that just got out of school with more debt than contacts. Jeremy Jones was a walking rolodex who was already working for millionaire corporate executives. He knew hundreds of them. Now all he had to do was get a few to join the hottest bank in the world during the hottest bull market the world had ever seen. Obviously it was a good hire and by the time 2010 rolled around, he would have built a team of seven, managing about 140 clients and $1.8 billion.

As a new Associate with no clients, I was always interested in how ultra-successful Private Bankers got their first client. I think it's says something about the business that most everyone will say that their first client was someone that they "knew." A family friend. A family member. An old boss. Jeremy Jones's first client was no different. It was someone that he knew. The interesting part is how this Private Banker that makes a lot of money for himself managed his very first client. After telling this person that he knew about his new job and getting him to fill out all the appropriate paperwork, Jeremy Jones's first client ever called in to do his first piece of business. He wanted to put in a buy limit order on a stock. Jeremy, who to this day doesn't place trades, told his assistant to put in the trade and left the office to go schmooze more millionaires.

Later that day, Jeremy got back to the office and his very first client ever was furious because he just lost $300,000. A buy limit order is one that can only be processed at or lower than the stated price. However, Jeremy's assistant put in the order as a market order: much higher than where the client had indicated. It was Jeremy and the assistant's fault that this happened. And, normally when this occurs, the Private Banker has to pay for the mistake. Since he was making nowhere near that kind of money yet, Goldman ate the whole thing: all $300,000 of it. The client is no longer with Jeremy Jones.

Goldman could easily have fired Jeremy Jones for this mistake, but they didn't and it was absolutely the best decision. Jones would make up for the loss exponentially over the next thirteen years.

As time passed, firms would recognize the value of Private Bankers and their millionaire and billionaire clients. Private Bankers would become a very hot commodity. So much so that in 2007–2010, the Great Recession, these Private Bankers would be the most hotly sought after employees on Wall Street and garner massive bonuses as the rest of the Street was losing money and firing people. Private Bankers and their clients were still generating a stable revenue stream and poaching clients from firms that no longer existed such as Lehman and Bear Stearns. The disruption in the market and failing firms created the perfect storm for guys like Jeremy Jones to make a lot of money.

Even though Jeremy Jones was working at Goldman Sachs, the story of his $11 million signing bonus begins at Lehman Brothers.

Remember that before Major Major Cooper was at Credit Suisse, he was running the Lehman Brothers office. And, yes, it was in the exact same building that Credit Suisse and Goldman Sachs currently reside. The building is like the home to a Private Banking soap opera full of bankers hopping from one firm to the next: a financial Melrose Place. Cooper began talking to Jeremy Jones when he was at Lehman, but could never get him to move. Why not? Lehman wasn't in the game of shelling out millions for fancy stockbrokers. Lehman went bankrupt in September 2008, and Cooper joined Credit Suisse in October 2008. It took him fourteen months to convince Credit Suisse to pony up the money and bring over Jeremy Jones. It was Major Major Cooper's big move. The thing he would live and die by. He needed to grow the office's assets and poaching from Goldman Sachs was a great way to do it. At the end of 2010 Major Major Cooper would put in his numbers for the end of the year and report millions of new assets flowed into the office. Of course they did. He paid millions for them. Who couldn't have made that deal? The interesting questions are how do you arrive at the $11 million number and what is the net present value of Major Major Cooper's deal?

The first component of the perfect storm for Jeremy Jones's $11 million is Major Major Cooper's move to a firm willing to pony up the millions. Lehman wasn't. Credit Suisse was. The next vital component was the market return of 2008. In 2008, the S&P 500 was down 37%. Whatever assets under management Jeremy Jones had at the beginning of 2008, he had about one third of that at the beginning of 2009. And, that's just market returns. You have to consider clients leaving. Jeremy Jones had clients in Global Alpha–the hedge fund that blew up. When these things happen, clients leave. When the markets are bad and your assets under management are dropping because your investments are dropping, then you start to think about leaving and turning your big list of clients into instant cash. Fortunately, in 2009, teams were being poached left and right. Big firms were disappearing and brokers were at least still making revenue as opposed to investment bankers that were losing money for firms. It was a perfect opportunity to pay someone a big bonus and have them bring over their millionaire/billionaire clients who provide the bank with a steady stream of fees year in and year out.

The way firms would calculate poaching bonuses was to take the all the revenue that all the broker's clients paid in the past year before the revenue is split between bank and broker and then put a multiple on that number. Multiples would range between 1.5x and 3.3x. Credit Suisse offered Jeremy Jones about 2.5x. The 2.5x is a funny number to me because it is the exact same mark-up number that retailers put on jewelry. It was like Major Major Cooper was purchasing some gold earrings for the office. Jeremy Jones, the Tiffany's of stockbrokers.

In 2009 Jeremy's clients paid Goldman about $4.4 million in total fees. A little over one million went to Jeremy Jones and the rest went to Goldman. So, Major Major Cooper starts trying to poach Jeremy Jones in 2009 and says we'll pay you 2.5 x $4.4 million: $11 million. We are still in a recession, Jeremy's revenues are still down. Goldman Sachs is being called into hearings before Congress. Now's the time to cash in on all those clients that you brought in over the years. Take the money. Anyone would have done it.

Within 3414 Peachtree's dramatic Melrose Place community of brokers hopping from one firm to the next, this was the biggest bonus ever paid. But getting employees from Goldman was nothing new. In fact, at the time Jeremy Jones came over there were twenty-five Private Bankers in the Credit Suisse office. Thirty-two percent of them had come from Goldman in the past five years.

The last thing I wanted to know about him was how he manages money. He told me that he doesn't place any trades. He does zero investment research. He acts as an intermediary. He takes money from millionaires and gives it to Separately Managed Account managers to do all of the investing. And, he has all of his assistants do the reporting and dealing with the money managers. He is rarely at his desk because his job isn't tied to the market. He's like Matlock, but with clients. I'll never forget the one piece of advice he gave me. He said, "W.E. I don't know why you go after people that only have $1 million. If their account drops to $800,000 then you lost them a lot of money and they will leave you. If you go after people with $25 million and their account drops to $20 million then they are still rich." I suppose that's the mindset you have after working in a decade where you didn't make any money in the stock market and put clients in hedge funds that blew up. Even though he was the big fish in the office, after he said that I knew that I never wanted to be that kind of Private Banker. I wanted to be more like Alex Finn and Bruce Lee: a great investor.

CHAPTER TWENTY-THREE

Separately Managed Accounts: A Rich Man's Mutual Fund

The Separately Managed Account is, from what I've been able to find, a thing that was created in the 1970's. When people begin to describe a Separately Managed Account, most will liken it to a mutual fund where an investor actually owns the stocks or bonds. The SMA is different than a mutual fund because a mutual fund actually owns the stocks and bonds and the investor owns a share of the fund. The main benefit that people who sell SMAs will point to is that since you own the actual shares, it is more tax efficient than a mutual fund. The SMA manager has more flexibility over offsetting gains with losses. It's a pretty simple thing to understand. Just think to yourself that this is a mutual fund where the investor actually has the stocks and bonds in his portfolio. Just think to yourself that this is a rich man's mutual fund.

These types of accounts were designed with a similar thought in mind as mutual funds: take your broker out of the loop. Instead of your broker buying stocks and bonds for you, your broker gives the money to someone else to buy the stocks and bonds. The broker makes a fee, but has no say in anything that the SMA manager buys and sells. The broker can check in every once in a while, but that is it. The relationship is just like a mutual fund. You don't trust yourself and you don't trust your broker, so put the money in the hands of others whom you do trust.

You've probably guessed one of the parties giving money to SMA managers-- Private Bankers who are putting their client's money with these managers. So, it's rich people that are investing in these. However, it wasn't always high net-worth individuals. Originally, it was institutions. In the world of investing in things that normal people can't, there are two types of investors.

Institutions and High Net-Worth Individuals. Institutions that have a lot of money they need to invest (think Yale Endowment) will not put money in a mutual fund. Endowments don't own Fidelity Magellan. Endowments give the money to SMA managers that will build portfolios that meet the Endowment's needs where the shares reside with the Endowment. The original thinking was that Endowments are so big with billions of dollars that they can easily afford to do this. They don't need to comingle their big boy money with the likes of small investors. They can keep it separate, demand a lot of special attention from the SMA manager, and keep it more flexible than a mutual fund. As the market moved from the stockbroker pitching stocks to Private Banking and fee based accounts, these types of investments were marketed to the high net-worth client.

About a decade ago, Private Bankers would start saying, "Now you can invest like Yale. Now you can have some more tax efficiency. These managers are only available to institutions and high net-worth. They are exclusive." It made sense and it had cache. So, SMA managers for the high net-worth client started to rise and rise. Using Maude's Factiva popularity contest search, here's what I found.

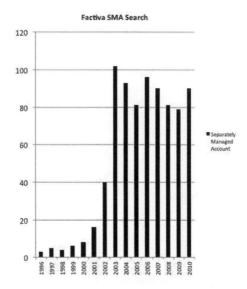

Just as Private Banking and Wealth Management were becoming popular, so were SMA accounts To me, it makes sense. The Separately Managed Account managers needed to sell their services to more people and they didn't want to do any cold calling on the rich because they have only been accustomed to calling on institutions. Technology made it easier for a smaller investor to use an SMA from a back-office standpoint, so instead of needing $10 million minimums from endowments to do this work, the managers entered the Private Banking market and asked for somewhere in the neighborhood of $250,000 minimums for an investment. And, for a $250,000 investment, an investor would have to pay the manager 2% per year. That's the deal that SMA managers made with Private Bankers. 2% became the basic entry level fee, but as account size grows, fees shrink. You saw what a portfolio of ETFs in a discretionary account would look like. What does an account of nothing but separately managed accounts look like? Here's an example:

DOMESTIC 80%		INTERNATIONAL - 20%	
Domestic Large Cap (75%)		International Developed (100%)	
Natixis AIA S&P 500	40%	Gratry & Company	50%
Morris Large Cap			
Growth	30%	Schafer Cullen	50%
Scott and Stringfellow	30%		
TOTAL	100%	TOTAL	100%

Domestic Mid/Small Cap (25%)	
Scott and Stringfellow	100%

All of the above names are SMA managers. And, each one of these managers would buy approximately thirty to fifty stocks for the portfolio. Since there are six managers listed above, the portfolio above would have about one hundred eighty to three hundred stocks in it at any given time. The number of stocks each managers chooses, thirty to fifty, is pretty much the standard for SMA managers and comes from the statistic that owning thirty to fifty stocks will diversify away any non-systemic or what is called company specific risk. Basically, statistics have shown that this is a good number of stocks to use to build a portfolio and everyone follows the idea. If the above portfolio were a $5 million or below account, then the investor would pay about 2% in fees: $100,000. Imagine having a relationship with this client for twenty years. That's $2 million in fees if the portfolio just stays at $5 million. About 60% of the fees go to the manager and 40% go to the Private Bank. Then, the Private Bank keeps about 65% of its fees and gives 35% to the Private Banker. Of the $100,000 above, $60,000 would go to the manager, $26,000 would go to the Private Bank, and $14,000 would go to the Private Banker.

I know you're thinking that $14,000 isn't a lot for the Private Banker to make every year, but if the Private Banker gets 40 clients exactly like the one above, then they are making $560,000 per year. That's not bad for giving money to someone else to manage. And, this is guaranteed year over year pay for the Private Banker as long as the clients don't leave. If the assets appreciate, then the Private Banker makes even more money. In the above scenario, the bank would make $1,040,000 guaranteed money year over year. No wonder banks are paying big bonuses to Private Bankers. Their clients generate tons of guaranteed cash with very little effort. Stockbrokers would have to place tons of trades and outperform their peers to make that kind of money. Maybe a stockbroker could crush it one year, but certainly his revenues weren't guaranteed like a Private Banker's. Because of fee based accounts, Private Bankers can now really make a lot of money.

In the above scenario, I was being very generous with assuming that a Private Banker's entire book of business would be paying 2% fees. Typically, a Private Banker will have a wide variety of clients; some smaller ones that will pay 2% and some bigger ones that will pay maybe .35%. All in all, I would say a good blended rate for someone like a Jeremy Jones is about 0.80%.

When you are like Jeremy Jones, and your clients have about $1,400,000,000 in assets, then the fees are smaller.

You can imagine how much work it would be for a Private Banker to manage $1.8 billion using only Discretionary Managed Portfolios. The Private Banker would be constantly tied to their desk and work weekends (think Alex Finn). Someone like Jeremy Jones who uses SMA managers never has to be in the office because he places no trades. Jeremy Jones is one man with three assistants who manage the SMA account managers: everyone else on his team is out schmoozing. He would have to be at his desk all the time if he managed all that money himself. He's actually out of the office more than he's in the office and probably prefers it that way. So, the only way for him to make his business work is to give the money to other people to manage. This type of business is scalable if you are the one man that is never in the office.

Another argument I've heard from Private Bankers who use SMA managers is, "I can't fire myself." This means that if the client's portfolio is underperforming, all the Private Banker has to do is fire one of the SMA managers. The Private Banker's argument is, "don't fire me I wasn't making the trades." I think that argument is ridiculous. The Private Bankers that use SMA should at least admit that they use them because they are not as good at managing money as the SMA managers. And, if the Private Banker isn't good at managing money and can't even pick other people that are good at managing money, then in my opinion the Private Banker should be fired.

CHAPTER TWENTY-FOUR

Getting Meetings

After almost getting the Jamaican as a client and almost getting the man that I met in the elevator as a client, the next few months were like a volatile stock with new highs and 52-week lows. I was all over the place. I was two months into my twenty-four month window for bringing in $40 million and I had brought in zero. Zero point zero, in fact. I had sat in the same room with millionaires. I had presented the firm to millionaires. I had presented to millionaires with one of the most senior Private Bankers in the firm. I had phone calls with millionaires, sent them letters and emails. After all of my hustling and pitching, no one filled out any new account forms or sent me any money to invest.

I told myself that I was at least building my pipeline--a list of people that might open accounts--but would need some time and work before anything happens. Without any clients to speak of, my life was spent prospecting. At times it felt like I was panning for gold: sifting through names and contacts until I found some possible pay dirt. Moving from location to location looking for a hot spot. As a Credit Suisse Private Banker, I wasn't just confined to Atlanta. So, I started to branch out to other parts of Georgia, North Carolina, Florida, and Kentucky. I would start by reaching out to people that I knew and then reaching out to people I didn't know to put together enough meetings to justify a trip.

To put together a good trip with a lot of meetings with CEOs and business owners, I would need to meet with people I had never met before. So, I was back to getting clients the old fashioned way: cold calling. I would look for "money in motion" what Private Bankers call money that someone just got and hasn't been invested yet. This is typically from selling a business or doing an IPO. And, I would focus on certain industries.

Whenever I would begin a round of cold calling I liked to think about Bruce Lee out of the Chicago office. If Bruce Lee cold calls you, you answer right? Brilliant. I'm changing my name to Chuck Norris. Cold calling in the south would be so much easier if I just had a name like Chuck Norris. I imagine people would take my call every time instead of hanging up on me or secretaries calling me Dubyah Eee from Credit Suzy. This seriously happened to me. I was called Dubyah Eee from Credit Suzy by a secretary. I really wanted to say, "Forget it lady, just tell Mr. CEO that I'm Chuck Norris from Bank of America." That was definitely one of my 52-week lows.

After hundreds upon hundreds of names and phone calls, I would eventually put together trips to North Carolina, Florida and Kentucky. I took my schmoozing on the road. My main focus on these trips was gaming and life sciences companies. Every young Private Banker has their niche market that they prospect and those were my two big categories. I certainly did not limit myself to only those two sectors, but I paid them the most attention. I had my reasons. First, and I hate to say it but it is true, Private Bankers riff off of their family. Bud Fox did it. Matlock would never shut up about his dad. And, even though my dad was unemployed, he had worked in the games business. Therefore, I had a slight connection to games and more knowledge than the average person. Second, my best friend's dad had made hundreds of millions starting and selling biotech companies and selling patents to drugs he invented. Because of him, I knew a little about biotech as well. I know what you are thinking. Why didn't you just sign your best friend's dad and be set for the rest of your life? He was just too close to me to go after. I didn't want to have to work for him and change the relationship. Besides, he really didn't have a need. Need is everything.

I would begin each of my trips by renting a Prius for about $60/day. I wanted to keep Major Major Cooper happy and keep my expenses down. I would buy a book on tape and drive around free of the office and cold calls and the stares of other Private Bankers in the office wondering how many more months were left until my salary was up and I would leave and reduce their competition. I was a man on the road.

One thing I quickly learned is when picking up a CEO at their office for a lunch meeting, the CEO expects you to drive. Every single time I met with a CEO and then went out to eat, they would say, "where did you park?" Then, I would drive us to the restaurant. I wanted to say, "Mr. CEO, a Private Banker in a rented Prius isn't going to lose you money. I'm conservative and cheap!"

My trips were whirlwinds filled with an assortment of food and drinks and executives of the south. Louisville was Galt House bourbons, Heine Brothers coffee, Jack Fry's, Safron's, Proof, non-profit fundraiser lobster, family office CEOs, philanthropists, foundations, and public company execs. Rubbing elbows with Whiskey execs, Tobacco Execs, and Hospital Execs and massive family offices. That's Louisville from the eyes of a Private Banker. Throw in a little Derby Pie from the Homemade Ice Cream and Pie Kitchen and life is good. Florida was Grease Burger in West Palm, Mario's in a strip mall in Daytona Beach near Tropical Tattoo (classy), Thai Sushi America in Eustis ($10 all you can eat sushi and I didn't die), Panera coffee in Lake Mary, Atlanta Braves Spring Training, amusement park toy distributers, amusement park game makers, amusement park ride makers, pharma companies, med tech companies, biotech companies and one real estate investment trust. Florida, got to love the culture of no culture. North Carolina was bio and barbecue. Bullock's BBQ, The Pit BBQ, Carolina Ale House, Durham, Raleigh, Chapel Hill, med tech, bio tech and video games. These trips were rich with food and executives of the south. Notice there were no yachts or drinking Chateau Margaux. These trips were a far cry from the fancy spoiled Private Banker I was in Switzerland. A far cry from Caduff's Wine Loft in Zurich and a bottle of Fleur de Pingus. However, each restaurant was representative of the region and so were the prospects. In Louisville it was whiskey, in Florida it was amusement parks and games, and in North Carolina it was biotech.

I kept my trips cheap. Private Bankers are supposed to preserve and grow money. Private Bankers are supposed to be conservative. For me, this comes natural. I'll rent a Prius and eat at a cheap barbecue joint every time. Sure I can fancy it up, but I cherish cheap lunches with millionaires in hole in the wall places. In Georgia, one of my favorite lunches of all time was with a millionaire biotech CEO at Weaver D's Fried Chicken in Athens. Automatic. For the People.

The outcomes of these first road trips as a Private Banker were relationship building or running into competition in the office. As a new Private Banker I always worried about calling the right people and not wasting time on bad prospects. One way to know that I was barking up the right tree was to call on and meet with people that other teams and bankers in the office were pursuing. There was a list that I was supposed to check to make sure this didn't happen but as a young Private Banker I was more concerned about being as active as possible and getting meetings. If I met with someone that another banker had already listed as their prospect on the list, then so be it. Coach wasn't going to yell at me for tackling too hard.

I realized this for the first time when I was in Louisville. I met with the head of one of the biggest family offices in the city. He was a friend of a friend and I met him in his office just to introduce myself and the firm. He told me in the meeting that he had met with one of the teams in the Atlanta office years ago. We chatted and I told him about myself and said that I would like to start a relationship and help if a need ever arises. It was just a simple introductory meeting. I was brand new to the business and told the guy what I was about. It took approximately one day for this meeting to get back to the team in the Atlanta office that was covering the family office. One of the younger guys in the family office was friends with one of the younger guys on the Credit Suisse team and basically said, "hey there's a guy from your company in here speaking with the head of the office." I quickly got an email saying "we have been covering them for over five years trying to do business with them. Back off. Don't you check the list?" I didn't check the list, but I felt good that I was at least knocking on the right doors. I knew that I wasn't going to get in any real trouble for it. The team that was covering the family office was the biggest team in Atlanta headed by a millionaire Private Banker of Jeremy Jones proportions. If that team couldn't do business with the family office in over five years, my chances were slim I would get there in less than two. I acknowledged their having listed the family office as a prospect and backed off. This would happen every once in a while but I always viewed it as a sign that I was prospecting the right people.

The majority of the trips were relationship building. I was brand new to the business so when I would meet with CEOs or business owners or lawyers or accountants, those first meetings were me telling them about myself and the firm to start to build a relationship. There was no way anyone was going to give me their millions to manage after just the first meeting. This was just a beginning. I would always leave with some sort of follow-up: provide them with research, investment analysis, introductions to investment bankers. My main way to keep in touch was to send out a two page summary that Weissenstein would create each month. Even if there was nothing to follow-up on, the least I could do to start a relationship was to send them the Chief Investment Officer's monthly statement to give them a sense of the firm's thoughts on the markets. It would give us something to talk about the next time we met. Most everyone I met with was open to that. Some would give me homework assignments and things to follow-up on: corporate account investment needs, bring back ideas for investments that are unique, introductions to the investment bank.

One thing that I will say separates a Private Banker from a stockbroker is the fact that we can make introductions to the Investment Bank and get paid a percentage of investment banking revenues if a deal transpires. If a Private Banker can do this it is like winning the lottery. The payout to a Private Banker for bringing in an IPO or a big leveraged loan can be in the millions. All for just making an introduction. All young Private Bankers dream of hitting upon this type of deal. It's like winning the lottery and I was not opposed to buying a few lottery tickets every now and then. Credit Suisse had a good biotech investment banking business and part of my prospecting strategy when meeting with CEOs of biotech companies that were portfolio companies of Private Equity firms was to offer them investment banking introductions. After a few months of making some pretty good introductions to the investment bank and getting them to fly down and meet with my prospects, I built a solid relationship with an Investment Banking Director. He would call me on my cell and always take my call. Having that connection was helpful in building relationships, but I never won the lottery.

Another way I would use my meetings to build relationships was to make introductions to Private Equity firms. Pretty much every Private Equity firm in the country has a bunch of just out of college kids from good schools calling on CEOs of private companies to find out about the business to make a possible investment. These kids scour the country looking for interesting private companies that meet their bosses' standards. One way to build relationships with Private Equity firms was to introduce them to private company owners that I had met with. I would make some good introductions and build a relationship with some Private Equity guys in hopes that if they ever sold or IPO'd a portfolio company they would introduce me to the people that would be profiting from the transaction. The "money in motion." Unfortunately, I never hit pay dirt.

What I did manage to do in those meetings and trips over my first few months was to strengthen relationships with people I already knew, meet millionaires I had never met before, build out my network, and get better at holding meetings. During those first few months, I built a strategy that would last me my entire time at Credit Suisse. I would do the first meeting alone and bring in Alex for the second meeting. He was an old guy that hadn't done any prospecting in years. It was a sight to see. Grandpa and I driving to meetings. I'm not quite sure he appreciated my indie rock radio station, but he was a good sport.

CHAPTER TWENTY-FIVE
Final Check

At the time of Final Check in New York, my last piece of the
training program, I was six months into my twenty-four month
window. I had been on a ton a meetings and conference calls. I had
new account docs with the Jamaican even though he had
disappeared on me. I was moving forward on a corporate account
with a Florida pharmaceutical company, I was accustomed to being
on my own and pitching new business. I had zero point zero in new
assets, but at least I wasn't embarrassing myself when I held
meetings and I think that's what Final Check was about. It was the
firm's way to make sure that after six months of on the job
hustling, you could sound intelligent on the phone and conduct a
meeting on your own. Like all Private Banking Training, I would
be given a case that needed me to reach out to other parts of the
firm to provide a solution. The case would be divided into a
prospecting phone call, a first meeting and a second meeting. The
meetings would be video-taped and there would be very influential
people sitting at a conference room with me at the top of One
Madison grading my performance. These graders were most likely
all millionaires in their own right. The cases were no cake walk.
Every single Associate from the year before me had failed. A
passing grade was a 70%. I will tell you this upfront, I might not
have had any accounts at this point, but I damn sure knew how to
hold meetings and do well on case studies.

Final Check was like a video game where I would have to fight
my way past different bosses to make it to the final boss so we
could have our ultimate showdown. The first boss would be the
head of the New York office, Matt Gorman, and my challenge was
to call him and get him to have a first meeting with me. This is an
elaborate way of saying that we were going to have a mock call.

Unlike all my previous cases I had to do in training, this one I would do alone. One young Private Banker trying to prove his skills in the top floors of One Madison.

Before flying to New York, I consulted Alex and we talked strategy. Basically we put together a game plan of how not to sound like a brand new banker. A portion of our strategy included a piece of the case that could use California Muni bonds, and we would use this to our advantage. I would continue to consult him during the case competition. He was my sensei, my rabbi, my Obi Wan. I was given a schedule with my case mapping out where and when I had to be. My first challenge would find me in a conference room in the upper levels of One Madison. I kind of wish it could have started on a lower level and then I could have worked my way up floors as I completed challenges, but I suppose that would have been a bit over-the-top.

As I exited the elevator on the floor of my first challenge, I noticed that there was no one there. I was early and the first one to arrive. I had all of my fire power with me: notes, research, and some probing dialogue I could use on the call if Gorman was being difficult. I laid out all of my materials and my notepad and practiced for twenty minutes. I probably looked like an idiot, but I wanted to make sure that the phone worked, and that my spiel sounded fluid and not completely rehearsed. I probably took it too seriously, but I even racked my brain as to whether I should call Gorman using the Polycom to speak hands free on the call or whether I should use the telephone and hold the receiver to my ear and talk. I practiced both. I was that serious about this. Everyone failed the year before and I loved a good challenge and wanted to win this thing. I chose to go with the telephone over the Polycom. That's how I had done the thousands of cold calls I made in the office. It felt more comfortable.

The call with Matt was easy. He didn't play hard ball like Weissenstein would have. The call was pretty tame and similar to this:

"Hi, Mr. Smith. This is W.E. Kidd from Credit Suisse. Your friend John said that I should give you a call."

"Sure. Tell me about yourself."

"I'm part of a team here that manages assets for families, foundations and entrepreneurs."

"Tell me a little about your firm. I've been getting a ton of these calls. What makes you different?"

Gorman was playing it like a textbook mock call. I had done a million of these six months ago and just glanced at my notes to rattle off why our firm was different. Then, I finished with the following:

"John said that you had told him you wanted to spend some time on your trust and estate planning. Let's find a time to meet and I can walk you through how we work with families who would like to update their estate plans."

He committed to the meeting and that was it. Very easy. That was day one. I had the rest of the day to spend preparing for the boss I would face the next morning. The next boss would be John Lloyd, the head of Separately Managed Accounts. Like all good games, the next level was much tougher. I spent the rest of the day creating a pitchbook, devising my strategy and practicing. First meetings are all about discovery. So, I made sure that I had my strategy mapped out and probing questions in my head and then met my buddy Northwestern Chicago at our favorite place to drink after work: Eleven Madison Park for a properly made Old Fashioned. A Credit Suisse case study was not complete if not followed-up with an Old Fashioned at Eleven Madison Park. We followed that up with some Momofuku Bar and called it a night. I was ready to tackle the next day's challenge.

The second challenge was much different. I arrived to the location early to get a feel of the space. It was what you would expect of a big conference room at a global bank. Long table.

Leather chairs. Conference room standard, except there was a video camera at the long end of the room. Credit Suisse definitely has some sort of voyeurism thing going on because we were constantly getting taped. I got there early so I could position the camera and chairs exactly where I wanted them. I assembled the chairs in such a way that John Lloyd would sit at the head of the table and then I could enter the room and sit next to him in a chair I had positioned so that it would be conducive for us to converse and not seem awkward.

Everyone trickled in: a woman that would tape the meeting (HR Lady), John Lloyd (mock client and head of Separately Managed Accounts), and Matt Gorman (Head of the New York Office and case grader). I was asked to exit the conference room and then reenter as if it were a real meeting. Fine, all for the sake of mockness. I walked back into the room and shook John Lloyd's hand and he introduced himself under his mock millionaire persona: Michael Bilsing. Michael was a friend of a friend and we established a few goals in our meeting. First, Michael had not formed an estate plan beyond wills. Second, Michael had some low cost basis stock that he wanted to monetize. Third, he wanted lending to purchase a vacation home. And, finally, he wanted to structure a balanced portfolio. I also found out that he had assets of $27 million. $10 million in a large cap equity portfolio, $16 million in restricted stock, and $1 million in cash. I got all of the information out of him by basically doing what I had seen Alex do in meetings. I just said, "tell me what you've been doing." We took it from there and I asked a lot more questions to be certain I had something to come back and present in the next meeting, but for the most part John was reasonable and I did a good job in playing the interviewee. I walked out of the room with a sense of what I needed to present in the second meeting to pass the test. As I was leaving, Matt Gorman said, "Hey W.E., I thought you did a good job." I about jumped out of my Hugo Boss shoes. This was unheard of praise in the world of Private Banking training.

I spent the entire rest of the day preparing for my third and final challenge. While the rest of my Associate class worked in the same cramped training computer lab, I brought my laptop and remote access key so that I could access the Credit Suisse intranet from my hotel. I sat in my underwear watching the World Cup on the massive flat screen in my hotel room and for the next eight hours straight worked my tail off. I knew the communal setting of the computer lab would just slow me down and I didn't want everyone to see that I was actually putting a ton of work into Final Check. Plus, if I could sit in my underwear with the World Cup on then why not?

I began sending emails and scheduling conference calls throughout the day and night for experts in the bank to help me present my solution to the case. Restricted stock was easy. I had already done this in Zurich. A quick call to Joe Leo's derivative team was all I needed to get numbers. Then, I could plug those numbers into the Variable Prepaid Forward model and slides I put together in Zurich and luckily saved. Lending was painless as well. I emailed our lending desk to set a time for a conference call and the actual call was very quick and just involved getting a rate. The big trick here was to make sure I pointed out that there were two pieces to the lending story. First, I had to get the cost of a non-purpose loan. I was quoted L+1.5%. Second, I had to point out that the yield on the collateral would be 1.75%. I was going to use muni-bonds as the collateral for the loan. So, the client would be making 1.75% and paying 1.85%. That was it. It would literally only take up one page of my deck. Trust and Estate and Portfolio Management took the most time as it is my weak point. I always made my buddy Northwestern Chicago handle that stuff in training. So, I spent about half an hour on a call with a trust and estate lawyer at the firm. She was tough to schedule on such short notice, but I needed her or else I was dead on that portion of the case. After walking the attorney through the mock client's situation an family we decided these were the structures I needed to address:

Revocable Living Trust, Irrevocable Living Children's Trust, Irrevocable Life Insurance Trust, and Charitable Remainder Trust.

The Portfolio Structuring piece was time consuming because it involved using the firm's software and entering a lot of data. Since I was going to be pitching the head of Separately Managed Accounts, I was going to have to use Separately Managed Account managers in my portfolio. This is something that I had never done, so it was going to take a little more time to pick managers and learn their fees and holdings. I structured the portfolio using all the top equity managers that John Lloyd himself had studied for years before allowing Private Bankers to offer them to clients, but I didn't pick any debt managers. The debt piece was my Trump card: my way to really impress the grader. In the first meeting, we had discussed that Michael Bilsing didn't have any bonds and with California's high taxes he wanted me to show him a muni bond piece in his portfolio.

So, my last step was to call a muni bond trader in California that Alex used. He was amazing. He put together some great materials for me, built a laddered muni bond portfolio, emailed it over and gave me his opinion of California as a credit. I told him I had a feeling I was going to get grilled on this and asked if he would mind me conferencing him in from the Polycom in the meeting room to make it feel like a real prospect situation. I gave him the approximate time that I would call and he said that he was game. I had a feeling I would get grilled on the munis because there was so much information on the page of bonds we were recommending: YTM, YTC, TEY. The rule is that if you give someone a piece of paper with numbers on it, then you better know what every number means. The muni bond page had numbers all over it and it was exactly what John Lloyd would try to trip me up on. It was pretty late by the time I put everything into a PowerPoint presentation. Twenty-five slides. Not too bad. I hate putting in too many slides. I got some dinner by myself and went to bed early: focused on crushing it in the morning.

My final meeting with John Lloyd/Michael Bilsing was set up exactly like the first, except this time instead of Matt Gorman watching from the far end of the conference table, it was Hugh Neuberger the head of Hedge Funds and Private Equity. I introduced my four topics: Trust/Estate, Lending, Restricted Stock Monetization, and Portfolio. I saved Portfolio for last because I knew I could fly through the first few sections without John pressing me too hard. Since he was the head of Separately Managed Accounts, he wouldn't grill me on the first three sections as long as I sounded intelligent and proved that I was prepared. He would definitely grill me on the portfolio and I was ready to lay my muni bond trap once we got there.

As I had guessed, the first three sections went quickly and the time I spent on conference calls and practicing the day before paid off. I was happy to finally be able to cover Trust/Estate on my own. As I began showing John Lloyd/Michael Bilsing how I structured the portfolio, I shied away from showing him the managers I had picked and highlighted that I allocated a portion of the portfolio to muni bonds as we had spoken about in the last meeting. Then, I showed him the page that included all the bonds that we had selected. I handed the page to John and his eyes lit up. The grilling began. What's this mean? What's 14@10? What's the difference between all these bonds? Education, water, why these? I smiled to myself. Yes…he fell for it. I really hoped that the trader was there when I dialed him. I said, "Well, Michael, I had anticipated your questions and have our muni bond desk in California standing by to walk you through the bonds and why we are using them. Let me dial him in." This was a huge gamble. If the trader didn't answer I was going to look like a fool.

The phone rang three times before the trader picked up. My lifeline. I explained all the questions we had on the bond portfolio and the trader breezed through all the answers like a true expert that had been doing nothing but trading muni bonds for the past ten years. I asked John Lloyd/Michael Bilsing if he had any more questions. He didn't of course. He looked at me as if to say, "you sneaky bastard I can't believe you just did that." I thanked the trader for his time and pressed the off button on the Polycom. I'm almost positive no one has ever done that in their Final Check, but it is something we do in real meetings all the time. It proved to be effective in my mock meeting and showed that I could truly handle myself and wouldn't embarrass the firm when meeting with prospects: the whole point of the Final Check.

I finished the presentation, describing the asset allocation and managers that I chose. Some minor grilling ensued, but after getting this far in the presentation without a blemish, I was fine with that. John Lloyd's expertise was Separately Managed Account Mangers and we danced back and forth with questions about top holdings of each manager, fees, and tax efficiency. I got beat up a little on tax efficiency, but I had never pitched a Separately Managed Account Manager to anyone in real life and I was bound to slip up a little. In the end, I was able to convince John Lloyd/Michael Bilsing to fill out new account paperwork. That was my goal and I accomplished it. I walked out of the mock meeting knowing that I had just passed my Final Check, something that no one did the previous year. I took a cab over to Torrisi Italian Specialties for a celebratory sandwich and a beer, then cabbed it over to LaGuardia. I was heading back down south.

All the other Associates found out about Final Check scores from their manager, but I found it particularly amusing that Major Major Cooper would never tell me my score. After everyone in my class had their scores, I asked Major Major Cooper a couple of times if he would tell me my score, but he kept dodging in true Major Major fashion until the head of the Philadelphia office called me and waked me through my performance. I had passed with a score of 86, one of the highest of my class. Matlock of course had failed. He would have to retake Final Check all over again via video conference, but by the second go round graders don't care and want to stop wasting their time and will pass anyone. Training was officially over.

CHAPTER TWENTY-SIX
Jake Moore

I don't expect anyone reading this to know the name Jake Moore. He is the protagonist in *Wall Street II*. I know I reference *Wall Street* a lot, but one way you can tell how prolific Bud Fox is is to type his name into any search engine. The character from Wall Street comes up every time. We've already established that Bud Fox was a stockbroker. It was pretty easy to watch the movie and see that. The same is not true of Jake Moore.

Even though Jake Moore is a self-proclaimed prop trader in the movie, we never see him place one trade for his company. In fact, the only prop trade that is even in the movie is Jake Moore telling his prop trader friends to place a trade which they profit from, but he does not make himself. I have a hard time believing Jake Moore is a prop trader because he never prop trades anything ever in the whole movie. The first thing that we see Jake Moore do business wise in the movie is to tell a scientist CEO that he is raising money for his solar power company that he himself has made a personal investment in. This would make you think that indeed Jake isn't a prop trader, but an investment banker trying to raise money for a solar power company. In the whole movie the only work that Jake Moore does is to try and raise money for a this company.

And, herein lies the issue with Oliver Stone *Wall Street* movies. The protagonists aren't ever tied to one job on Wall Street. The protagonists *are* Wall Street. Bud Fox was a stock broker and a hostile take-over banker. In the 80's that was cool on Wall Street. Bud Fox took on multiple Wall Street personas to the point that it was a little far-fetched. The same goes for Jake Moore. Maybe he's a prop trader or a hedge fund guy or a private equity guy or an investment banker. He takes on all those personas because he is everything on Wall Street jammed into one person. After watching the movie I was thinking to myself that the whole solar power storyline was ridiculous, but then I went down my own Jake Moore solar power rabbit hole.

Shortly after Final Check, I was sitting at my desk one early morning, drinking coffee and searching headlines for money in motion. IPOs announced, companies sold, patents licensed, etc. I would typically search 10 – 20 news sites every morning. On this particular day I came across a headline for a solar power company that had just broken ground on a new solar farm. It was a little serendipitous because a week before a group within Credit Suisse Private Banking had flown down to the Atlanta office and presented on how they were our connection to the Investment Bank and gave us some examples of deals Private Bankers have done with the investment bank. Most of these deals were complicated large leverage loans for family owned firms. Imagine a $100 million dollar loan to family that owns a coal mine.

The part of the presentation that caught my attention was that the payouts to the Private Bankers were in the range of $600,000 to $1 million, just for making one introduction. Six hundred grand just for an introduction! I've said it once and I'll say it again. There's no justice in the world. The group said that they were currently interested in project finance loans for renewable energy companies. I introduced myself to the group and said I would start looking for deals for them. I couldn't help but walk out of the room with daydreams of big dollar deals. One week later, the article about a solar farm looked very promising.

My first step was to lob a call into the CFO of the Solar Power company. I got his voicemail. Getting voicemail or a Natalie/secretary is industry standard for a young Private Banker. You rarely ever get anyone just by making one call. I decided to leave a message and to my surprise the CFO returned my call the next day. After two years of cold calling and leaving messages, only twice has anyone ever returned my call. A CEO of a local company and now this CFO. After introducing myself and the firm's appetite for project finance, the CFO sent over some materials on a project they were working on that was looking for a $100 million project finance loan. I reviewed the documents and before sending it to the team that connected us to the investment bank, I wanted to make sure that the company met a few criteria. I had to determine that it was profitable, that it had a track record and that the project was big enough to pique the interest of our investment bankers. These three criteria are rarely met when speaking to small, privately owned companies, but this company looked legitimate with a legitimate project. So, I sent the documents to the team that connects Private Bankers to Investment Bankers and set a time for us to have a conference call with the CFO.

Alex and I would conference in the CFO and our intermediary man and walk through the proposal together. It was my deal that I brought in, but when our intermediary man began talking to the CFO about megawatts, giga watts, photovoltaic systems, plant specifications and site evaluations, I was lost. It was exactly like the part in *Wall Street II* where the screen turns into a digitized energy facility and the audience just accepts what the movie says as true. I had no idea about renewable energy specifics, but I accepted what was being said and hoped it was enough to get us a meeting with the investment bankers. Luckily, it was. I just helped open the call, move it forward, and acted as intermediary. Whatever was said, it was good enough to pique the interest of the head of Leveraged Finance for all of Credit Suisse because we were now set to have a conference call with him. This was getting serious.

It was shortly after this that the CEO / Russian Scientist of the Solar Power company called me on my cell phone and thanked me for setting up the meeting. That was my Jake Moore moment. The very first scene in *Wall Street II* shows Jake Moore going to work on his motorcycle when the scientist of a Renewable Energy company calls him on his cell phone about raising capital. And, that just happened to me. I thought it was ridiculous in the movie and now it just happened to me. I couldn't believe it.

I wasn't a prop trader like Jake. I was a Private Banker. In the world of Private Banking, these unlikely moments occur because of the nature and complexity of the clients that Private Bankers prospect for and work for. If Jake Moore was a Private Banker, the movie would have made more sense. So, Oliver Stone, if you are reading this, take note. A Private Banking character would give you the flexibility to roam all over the spectrum of Wall Street jobs. From Investment Banking to home loans, Private Bankers are involved. From IPO stock distributions to buying stocks and bonds, Private Bankers are involved. From structuring a Trust to hedging restricted stock for the CEO of a publicly traded firm, Private Bankers are involved. Private Bankers take on the most personalities on Wall Street because wherever there is a millionaire, there is a Private Banker.

The conference call with the head of Leveraged Finance and the CFO of the Solar Power company went much like the first conference call. I acted as quarterback and made introductions, then let the head of Leveraged Finance and the CFO hash it out. The call lasted an hour and afterward I thought it could go either way. There was a 50/50 chance I was going to be rich just for making an introduction, which is every Private Banker's dream.

At this point it was out of my hands. All I could do was wait and see if Leveraged Finance wanted to do the deal. After a couple of days, we got word that the deal wasn't going to move forward. Apparently, the sources of cash to pay back the loan were too heavily dependent on government grants and the government was moving very slowly on paying them. I didn't feel too awful about it. All of us knew it was a long shot. Come to think of it, Jake Moore was never able to raise the money for his Solar Power company on his own. He needed his future wife and father-in-law to give the money to his Solar Power Company. That's the one similarity Bud Fox and Jake Moore have, they both needed to leverage their family. That's one of the most interesting connections between the two movies.

I still keep in touch with my little Solar Power company. I've been to their plant and met with the CEO/Scientist. I tried to get him to open a Private Banking account, but he was more focused on people giving him money than giving money to people.

This wasn't my only attempt to get an investment banking deal done. I would establish a relationship with our Healthcare Investment Bankers in New York and have them fly to Atlanta to meet with biotech portfolio companies that I introduced them to. I would meet with hospitals and pitch them on our Healthcare Banking team's advisory and capital raising strengths. I always thought I was close to closing a big deal, but it never happened.

One day in February 2011, I opened up *The Wall Street Journal* to learn that Kindred Healthcare had just bought RehabCare Group for $900 million. Kindred was advised by Morgan Stanley on the deal, but I was in Kindred meeting with them ten months prior to the closing of the deal. What if they asked me to make an introduction to our Healthcare Investment Bankers? What if we ended up doing the deal instead of Morgan Stanley? I think this mentality is something that is inherent in the life of a young Private Banker. I call it the "jam tomorrow" mentality.

Lewis Carol invented the phrase "jam tomorrow." It's in the *Through the Looking Glass and What Alice Found There*. I think it's an accurate expression to describe the experience of being a Private Banking Associate. As an Associate, you are not rich. Not even close. But there is a constant feeling that pervades your everyday that if the right person says "yes," then you could be set for the rest of your career. If that investment banking introduction turns into an IPO then you will make millions. The deal can fall apart or make you a millionaire. It's a feeling that haunts all

Private Bankers and I'm not sure if it motivates us to make that extra phone call or whether it turns us into foolish dreamers.

CHAPTER TWENTY-SEVEN

It's All In The Game

In addition to lofty dreams of one-time six or seven figure payouts, a Private Banker's life is fraught with small battles fought every day for prospects. There's a reason why I would search the news every morning for companies being sold or companies going public. The owners and major stock holders would receive huge liquidity events and need advice on how to manage their new found wealth. Private Bankers careers are made on taking advantage of such opportunities. Every day teams of Private Bankers around the country cull over news and then submit the names to the office manager to get the right to pursue the money in motion. If you are on a big team or have an introduction, typically you would get to be the person that would be chosen to call on the new money. Being a new Associate, I would submit for money in motion, but if anyone other than me had found the deal, then it would go to the more experienced person. So, I changed my strategy. I only submitted for the long shots that no one thought they had a chance of getting and opportunities no one else could find. Sometimes, I would attempt to guess what company I thought would be next to have a liquidity event and submit for it before it happened. I actually picked a handful of companies that way.

In June of 2010, I was searching the website sec.gov for recently filed S-1 documents. An S-1 is a document that a company must file prior to doing an IPO. One way that Private Bankers will prospect for money in motion is to search sec.gov every day to check for new IPOs and then call on the executives that will be profiting most from the IPO. On June 8· 2010, while searching sec.gov, I came across an S-1 for a company called FleetCor Technologies. The company was in the business of providing payment systems to large fleets of vehicles and they were not too far from our office. I submitted my name to Major Major Cooper to get the right to be the person from our office to prospect the executives. Goldman Sachs, JP Morgan and Morgan Stanley were taking the company public. My guess was that no one else in the office would submit for FleetCor once they saw who was doing the IPO. My guess was that everyone would think it was hopeless if all our competitors were doing the deal. I was right. A couple of days after submitting for FleetCor, I got an email saying, "no one else asked for this." I put the CFO of FleetCor on my list of people I would call every week and then I began trying to get a meeting.

I didn't go after FleetCor too aggressively. Even I knew that it was a huge long shot. A couple of weeks after I began calling on them , I noticed one of the guys on Jeremy Jones's team whispering to Major Major Cooper's assistant. Afterwards, Major Major Cooper's assistant came over to my desk and asked if I had gotten in contact with FleetCor yet.

"No. Why?" I asked.

"Because Jeremy Jones's team is going to try to get them. You should hurry."

I was just a new Associate with no clients and if Jeremy Jones wanted to go after a company that I submitted for, then nothing was going to stop him. If I complained, it would do no good. Major Major Cooper would just tell me to give it to Jones. So, I started to call the CFO of FleetCor like crazy to try to get a meeting. To my surprise, after many calls, the CFO picked up the phone. When calling on a CFO of a hot IPO being taken public by Goldman Sachs in the next few months, you don't ever expect the CFO to pick up the phone. However, you have to be prepared for the chance that he will because you will only get about three minutes maximum to convince him to meet with you.

Within three minutes, I hit all of my talking points. Absolutely nothing that I said had anything to do with investments. I spoke about Directed Share Programs, Hedging & Monetization Strategies and Equity Compensation Programs. Without getting into too much detail, suffice it to say that these three topics are front and center on a CFO's mind prior to an IPO. There is a group within Private Banking that specializes in these services. The group is called Corporate & Executive Services. The Private Banker rarely does anything themselves. There's always a group within the bank they have to use to get anything done. The Private Banker is just the front man. After my spiel, the CFO said, "Well, no one has spoken to me about Equity Compensation Programs yet. Let's set a call with your Corporate & Executive Services group."

I made Major Major Cooper's assistant aware of my progress and would go on to have an hour long conference call with FleetCor's CFO, our Corporate and Executive Services Group, and Alex. The CFO was focused mostly on Executive Compensation Programs and how we would manage a million dollars. A question that prospects always ask to gage how a Private Banker manages money is "If I gave you a million dollars, what would you do?" The Corporate and Executive Services Group fielded all of the Executive Compensation Program questions. Alex handled everything related to investments. And, I acted as moderator and helped move the call along and summarized everything that we covered. The CFO was very engaged during the hour we spent with him. I had offered him two of the best most experienced people at the bank to speak about how we work with clients. At the end of the meeting, we told the CFO the next step was to fly a few bankers in from New York and present the firm to all the executives in one meeting at FleetCor with Alex and I representing the Atlanta office. If we could get all the executives in one room and present it would be like striking gold. The CFO said he would let us know if he would like us to come in. He was planning on having a few banks present.

I thought that I had a decent chance of getting us into FleetCor to present to the executives and I thought that I just edged out Jeremy Jones's team. I thought that after having a successful conference call with the CFO and getting other parts of Private Banking involved meant that I was golden. FleetCor was my prospect. However, a couple days after our conference call, I got a curious email from one of the seven people on Jeremy Jones's team asking if we could talk for a minute. I knew immediately that FleetCor would be the topic. I walked over from my little cubicle in no man's land to Jeremy Jones's office. All seven of the Private Banker's that comprise his team sit in a glass encased office about twenty yards from my cubicle.

When I entered Jones's office the only people in there were an assistant and the Private Banker that sent me the email.

"What's up?" I asked.

"I just wanted to let you know that we've got one of the Board of Directors of FleetCor and he's introducing us to everyone else. I just wanted to do the mature thing and let you know. You're not mad?"

"No. I'm not mad," I replied. We were like two street thugs battling over turf: pawns obeying an unwritten rule of courtesy so we didn't have to get the boss involved.

As I walked out of Jeremy Jones's office I said, "It's all in the game."

I knew I didn't have the power to battle Jeremy Jones's team. The bank had to make back its millions and Cooper would do anything for them so it looked like he made a good decision in poaching them. Rarely do I ever sound cool or like a gangster, but I felt empowered as I walked out of Jones's office knowing I just riffed a line off of HBO's *The Wire*. I thought I saw Jones's assistant's ears perk up at the perfect reply. As I said it I couldn't help to recognize what a turf war it is to guard clients and prospects.

I would try to contact the CFO again many times, but he went radio silent on me. He wouldn't take my calls or return my emails. I was dead to him. It's all in the game. That's how we do.

Chapter Twenty-Eight

So You Want a Swiss Bank Account
(and you don't want to go to jail)

I promise this is the last time I'll mention *Wall Street II*. My favorite lines in the whole movie are between Jake and Gekko. Jake asks, "What would you do with your money?"

"Me?" Gekko replies thinking about how much truth he wants to divulge to Jake. "Switzerland. Still the best." He truthfully answers. If only Gekko were real I would give him a call. He's the perfect prospect, a millionaire that prefers Swiss banks.

This scene got me thinking. I worked at a Swiss bank and I had no idea how to open an account in Switzerland. If a client asked me to do this I would be lost. I knew it was possible. I also knew that the US Government had gotten UBS to divulge names of US clients and having a Swiss bank account became associated with illegal activity and not paying taxes. What if someone wanted to do it the legal way? Not long after hearing Gekko say that he kept all of his money in Switzerland, I found the answer.

If you open an account with UBS or Credit Suisse in the United States, you are opening a brokerage account. There's no mystique or romance associated with a brokerage account. If you open an account with UBS or Credit Suisse in Switzerland, then that's when the iconic images of Swiss Banks come rushing to the surface. For me I immediately think of James Bond, *The Bourne Identity*, *The DaVinci Code*, World War II, drug dealers, terrorists, and secrecy. I think it's the secrecy that really allows people to use their imaginations when imagining what a Swiss bank account is all about.

In my day to day of driving back and forth to work and cold calling, I have yet to run across a spy, person hiding the secret to Christianity, Nazi, drug lord or terrorist. But I was asked by a very conservative retired man how he could put $1 million in an account in Switzerland. He didn't want to do anything illegal, he said he would just feel safer if he had some money in Switzerland because he was starting to worry about the US Government.

I discovered that it is just about as easy to open an account in Switzerland as it is to open an account in the United States. Switzerland is just more expensive. Out of the fifty-two thousand employees at Credit Suisse, thirty-five of them cover Swiss Bank accounts for residents of the United States. In total they have about 1,000 accounts. So, in August of 2009 when UBS gave the IRS 4,500 names of United States residents with UBS off-shore accounts in Switzerland, you have to imagine that they pretty much gave away the names of a majority of their clients. Also note, that the 1,000 accounts I mentioned are most likely doing things by the book and I'm not going to get into the sneaky illegal stuff people can do.

To open a Swiss bank account at Credit Suisse from the comfort of your home in the United States, you start by having the team in Zurich send you new account paperwork. To get in contact with the team in Zurich, you could call them directly or have a Private Banker from the United States call them for you. You fill this paperwork out and mail the original forms and signatures with a copy of your passport to Zurich. Once Zurich gets the paperwork, it takes about three to four weeks to open the account. The head of the team told me that it takes so long because, "we must do background checks and we are very precise." Once the account is opened, you will then be given wire instructions to wire money into your account. That's it. As long as you are doing it the legal way, it is pretty easy. The opening of the account isn't much different than opening an account at any bank, but the fees and minimums are different.

The minimum size of the account is $1 million. Credit Suisse will not open up an off-shore account for a United States resident for less than that. For an account size of $5 million or more, Credit Suisse will throw in internet access so you can view your account online. You can't process any transactions online, but you can view your account online as long as you have $5 million or more.

The fees are a combination of custodial fees and transactional fees. Custodial fees are .25% per year and are only charged on securities held in the account. So, if you have an account in Zurich with $1 million of stock and bonds in it then, you are charged $2,500 per year just for the privilege of having it reside in Switzerland. You are also charged a transactional fee per trade. This is very much like how brokerage accounts were in the 80's. You are charged 1.8% per trade. So, if you want to buy $1 million dollars' worth of Apple Inc., then you will be charged $18,000 for that trade. Making trades in Zurich is a little more expensive than making them on E-Trade.

I couldn't help having a nostalgic 80's feeling at the thought of 1.8% fee per trade. Why can Zurich charge so much on an account? There's not too much competition. There's no Swiss Banking E-Trade out there for United States citizens. I couldn't imagine the Swiss government allowing such a thing.

The fact of the matter is that as the United States government's debt increases into infinity, the very rich are becoming concerned about the safety of their money. There are many United States citizens who have a Swiss Bank account at Credit Suisse that holds nothing more than gold. If you would like to open an account and hold nothing but gold and make no trades, then the fee is very small. Roughly $300/year. Personally, I think a United States resident opening an account in Switzerland to hold gold is like buying a Toyota Prius and then supping it up with bullet proof windows. You're already conservative. Now, you're just paranoid. However, people do open accounts in Switzerland and they pay for it. They pay for it in two ways. First, in increasing the complexity of their tax reporting to the IRS. And, second, by paying a lot more in transactional fees and custodial fees.

CHAPTER TWENTY-NINE

My First Account

My first account I ever opened was for someone that fits the definition of Ultra High Net-Worth Individual. I began prospecting the individual in November 2009 and didn't get a "yes" until November of 2010. The account itself wasn't opened until February 2011. When the account was opened, I felt a great sense of accomplishment. I was no longer playing Private Banker. I was a real Private Banker. I had a client.

The process of opening my first account began soon after getting back from Zurich/New York training. My first client, who I will name Mr. Big, is someone that would be impossible for a Private Banker to open an account for without some sort of an "in." I had an in. I've known Mr. Big for years. We've probably never spoken more than a few sentences to one another. And, I hadn't spoken to him in perhaps twenty years, but if I called him and said my name he would know who I was. However, I knew that calling him directly wasn't the way to go. I also had no idea of how to even get a phone number for the guy. Going directly to Mr. Big wasn't the answer because Mr. Big had a family CFO that ran his financial life. Big families will often have a family office. Arthur Blank, founder of Home Depot, has a family office of about thirty-five people that run his financial life. Mr. Big and his family had one family CFO running things. You would never know who he is because there's no sign over his door that says Family CFO, but I knew it was him that I needed to go through to get to Mr. Big.

During one of my first of many cold calling sessions in November 2009, I gave the Family CFO a call. After telling him about my new job, he said something to the effect of, "So you're one of those guys that takes my money, charges me a fee and tells me what to do."

I was a little shocked, but the more I thought about it, the more he was right. We did take people's money, charge them a fee and tell them what to do with their portfolio. Our marketing materials dress it up a bit more than that, but he was right. In fact, I think it's a very good definition.

The great thing about speaking to a family CFO is that instead of yammering and making small talk about golf or football or the weather, you can get right to talking about money.

"How do you invest?" I asked.

"Look," he says, "I've had Private Bankers pitch me and I've just never liked them. I don't like the 1% wrap fee. We use a financial advisor. Sometimes I use the financial advisor's advice, but I like to run my own money and just pay for the transaction."

He began telling me the types of investments that they were holding; they had everything. Stocks, Bonds, Private Equity, Hedge Funds, Structured Notes, REITs, even a few Separately Managed Accounts. I tried pitching him a few things, but every time I did he would say, "Yeah. We've already got something like that."

Fortunately, he did have a question. He was sitting on a lot of cash. Excellent, I thought to myself. He said, "I'm looking for yield. Any ideas?"

I pitched him Master Limited Partnerships.

"Yeah. We've got those. I don't like the K-1's. Think about it and come back to me with something low risk with more yield than my money market which is essentially zero."

"Okay. I'll put together a short duration high grade bond portfolio for you with a view that interest rates are bound to rise and we'll re-invest at a higher interest rate." At least, now I had a homework assignment.

Finding yield in January of 2010 was what everyone wanted to talk about. With interest rates at practically zero, the Fed was forcing investors to take on risk. Holding cash became un-American and penalized. I consulted with Alex and our bond desk and then Alex and I chose twelve bonds to include in the portfolio--$100,000 of each bond.

We constructed an analysis of the portfolio. Page one had a summary of the twelve bonds which had an average rating of A-, a duration of 1.27 years and a yield-to-maturity of 1.11%. None of the bonds were callable. Page two showed a summary of cash flows over time. That's the beauty of bonds when they don't default – you know exactly what you are going to get and when you are going to get it. On page three we showed a distribution of maturities and issuer types. It was a slick little three pager and we tried to sexy up our 1.1% laddered bond portfolio as much as we could, but in the end there is nothing attractive about 1.1%.

Alex and I did a conference call with the family CFO and walked him through the portfolio. His reaction was, "I'm not going to invest in corporate bonds for 1.1%, but I'm impressed with the presentation. I'm really impressed guys." In the end I always knew that my only goal on that call was to impress him. I knew he wouldn't jump at 1.1%. I was proud of the work that we had done. It reflected our philosophy of smart investing at a low cost. That bond portfolio would have cost the family CFO about $1,200 in fees (or $1 per bond) and it wouldn't have blown him up. All interest and principal would have been paid and would have given him a better return than the money market.

Impressing the family CFO was enough to earn me a lunch with Mr. Big's brother and son-in-law. And, I also got meeting with Mr. Big's daughter. This would occur on one of my whirlwind food filled road trips of the southeastern United States. I got grilled by the entire family. And, the family CFO just sat there and let them take shots at me too see how I would respond. It was the first time that the Weissenstein grilling had paid off. I didn't get flustered. The first thing that the daughter said to me when we met was, "So you're one of those guys that takes my money, takes a fee, and tells me what to do." It was exactly what the family CFO had said to me when we first spoke, and I got the sense that they had met with a lot of Private Bankers and would not do fee based accounts. She followed that up with, "Apple is up today. What should I do?" Apple was below $250 at that point and I told her that our analyst just raised the price target to $300. It was a good response even if it wasn't a definitive answer because by year-end Apple would have shot through $300.

The family would hit me with more questions, some of which I could answer and some of which I couldn't. "Is the dollar dead? What about inflation? What's with the healthcare bill? Can you provide financing for our business? Are we in a recovery? If I gave you one million dollars what would you do with it?" In addition to questions there were also some statements such as, "Next time you come back, I'll kill you if you wear a suit." And, "Would you look at this kid there's not a wrinkle on him." Through it all I kept my composure.

I pitched the firm and how we invest and our thoughts on the market. It was March 17th 2010. The S&P 500 was at 1166. I said we were bullish with a year-end target of 1300. We ended 2010 at 1257 and crossed 1300 on February 1st 2011. I said that we've seen earnings continue to beat expectations and expect they will continue to do so because expectations are so low. I said that math will eventually win over market psychology and when it does a 16x multiple on the S&P 500 earnings puts us at around 1300 for the year. In all honesty I was just reiterating Weissenstein. He was our god and I was preaching his gospel.

Once I was back at 3414 Peachtree I no longer pitched the family CFO on a fee based account and just stuck with individual investments. I tried an International Bond Portfolio, Muni Portfolio, Distressed Debt Private Equity. In between the pitching I would learn more about what they owned, which was practically everything. I would continue to check in with them once every couple of months and update them on our thoughts on the market. Thankfully, Weissenstein was spot on with his predictions. He was damn close to predicting the S&P 500 in 2010. He was overweight emerging markets, small cap, mid cap, and technology. He preferred growth over value. Alex and I listened and in Alex's accounts and in my prospecting meetings, we played it just like it was–the beginning of a recovery.

It was around November 2011 when I began pitching the family CFO a product that finally resonated: a Structured Note. This is a debt obligation issued by a bank that typically offers an investor a non-linear payoff structure. An investor will be given an offering memorandum that says if such and such happens we are obligated to pay you this and if such and such doesn't happen we are obligated to pay you that. The two risks are if such and such doesn't happen or if the bank goes bankrupt. If the bank goes bankrupt, the investor becomes a general creditor of the bank in bankruptcy court (this happened with Lehman Brothers). Banks will hedge the risk of offering structured notes by buying or selling securities and derivatives that match the terms of the note.

Let me give you an example of the structured note that resonated with the family CFO. The terms were that an investor would give Credit Suisse $100,000 per note. For that $100,000 Credit Suisse would pay the investor 8.5% per year over 18 months: coupons were paid quarterly. At the end of 18 months the investor would get the $100,000 back if the S&P 500 or Russell 2000 had not fallen by 35% or more. If the S&P 500 or Russell 2000 had fallen by 35% or more, then the investor would participate in the full extent of the loss experienced by the worst performing index.

Essentially, this note gives an investor an 8.5% coupon paid quarterly and some downside protection in case there is a market correction. There is one more twist to the investment. It is callable quarterly at par. As an investor, if the note was called you would get your coupon payment and $100,000 back which you could use to invest in another note with similar terms.

For you finance geeks out there that are wondering what the bank is doing behind the scenes to be able to offer such a note, they are basically buying a put on the S&P 500 and Russell 2000 on lay-a-way from the investor. The investor gives the bank $100,000 on day one and then the bank pays the investor 8.5% per quarter for the put-like structure. If the bank decides it is too expensive to continue to pay the investor the coupon for the put, then they will call the note.

The beauty of the note for the investor is that none of the options or securities are imbedded in it. The note is just a contract between the investor and the bank with specific terms. If your head is spinning, know that what I just described is probably the simplest of all Structured Notes. They can get very complex.

In the global casino of investing, if there is a game you want to play that isn't available, for enough money someone will structure the game for you. In late 2010 investors were still looking for yield and were cautious of a market correction. In order to supply investors with a way to act upon this view, banks began offering callable yield notes like the one described above. Personally, I liked to pay attention to the Structured Notes that we were offering. Because of my background in Asset Securitization, I found the notes to have a similar concept and thought that every once in a while I could find an interesting one. Most were too risky with unattractive structures, but I liked the simple short term notes like the 18 month callable yield note on the S&P 500 and the Russell 2000.

In November 2010 when the family CFO started to show some interest in the Structure Note, he emailed me and let me know that Mr. Big would be in town on November 16th. I made some phone calls to other people in Mr. Big's state, put together a trip of about eight meetings including Mr. Big and submitted it to Major Major

Cooper for approval. It took a year, but I finally got a meeting with Mr. Big.

On the day of my meeting with Mr. Big, I put on my suit and tie and headed to a coffee meeting and a lunch meeting, then drove over to Mr. Big's in the afternoon. As I sat in the parking lot about to meet with Mr. Big, I made a conscious decision to take off my tie and suit jacket since the family CFO said he'd kill me if I wore a suit and tie again.

Upon my arrival, I was met by the Family CFO. He was wearing a suit. Then, I saw the brother, the son-in-law and the daughter. They were all wearing suits.

"I took off my jacket and tie in the car. You said you would kill me if I came back in a suit," I said to the family CFO.

"Well...at least you listen. It's okay. You caught us on one of the few days a year we dress-up." The family CFO walked me over to see Mr. Big and as we approached him the family CFO joked, "I told him that next time we met I would kill him if he wore a suit. He listened." Mr. Big laughed.

The meeting with Mr. Big wasn't like anything that I had experienced in training. There was no grilling at all. I had about five minutes with Mr. Big. He listened more than he spoke.

"Tell him about the Private Equity deal and tell him about the Structured Note," said the family CFO.

I began with the Private Equity deal. Like all Private Equity deals, he would be a limited partner in the investment, but unlike most Private Equity deals, he would receive current interest and the investment would start repaying investors in year two with the intention of having all money paid back by year three. Most Private Equity deals have a timeline of ten years. I liked this deal because it was a relatively short period of illiquidity and it paid current interest of about 4% per year. The reason it paid current interest was because the general partner was investing in senior secured bank loans of distressed companies that the general partner expected would be repaid. After I finished describing the Private Equity deal, Mr. Big asked how many people worked at the fund.

"About thirty-five," I said.

"Feels like Madoff. I don't like it. What's the Structured Note?" asked Mr. Big.

Mr. Big had invested in structured notes in the past and was familiar with them, so my pitch was simple.

"8.5% coupon paid quarterly. 35% downside protection on the S&P 500 and Russell 2000. 18 month maturity."

Mr. Big turned to the family CFO and said, "Do you trust the kid?"

"Yeah. I trust the kid."

"Okay," said Mr. Big. He looked deep into my eyes like he was looking into my soul, pulled me in for a hug and whispered, "Don't lose my money, kid."

This was on November 16th 2010. The account wouldn't be opened until February 1st 2011. Like all accounts, there was a number associated with it. I had just opened my first numbered account at a Swiss Bank. Sure, it was onshore in the United States, but I couldn't help but think back to "The Numbered Account" book my grandmother bought me. She would be proud.

CHAPTER THIRTY

It's The Hardest Job There Is

By late February of 2011, my Associate class would be cut by 30%. Every Private Banking associate hire in the New York office would leave or get fired during the first year. There were only seven left of the ten that started in the United States. I liked to keep good-bye emails in my Outlook In-box as a reminder of fallen soldiers. The emails would sit there like tombstones reminding me how short the life of a Private Banker can be.

I had my first account open for Mr. Big and I had new account docs with three other prospects. All three prospects had given me a "yes" and just needed some time to fill out the forms and transfer assets. As I learned with Mr. Big, these things take time. The main similarity between all the accounts was that I had known all of them prior to becoming a Private Banker. It took me over a year to get some traction and start to make progress opening new accounts and now I just had ten months left. The clock was ticking and even though I had opened a new account, which hardly any new associates do, I didn't feel successful. I didn't know what was going to happen at the end of ten months either: it was something that was never mentioned.

There was one other associate in the office that had gone through the Global MBA training program. He was exactly one year ahead of me. He was the only associate in Atlanta to go through the global MBA training program and make it past two years. I felt like he was the only person in the office that could give me an idea of what my future entailed. We had never really spoken to each other much over my first year because Private Banking is for lone wolves. Since I never called on any of his prospects and he never called on any of my prospects, there was no reason for us to talk. We were more competitors than anything. He was on a team and his team sat in a big glass office similar to Jeremy Jones's. Everyone on teams got to sit in big glass offices with the rest of their team. Since I wasn't officially on a team, I was slumming it in the cube farm.

I shot the other associate an email and we walked across the street to Lenox Mall together to grab a coffee. It's amazing how suspicious two associates who aren't on the same team walking anywhere together look. Everyone stares at you as if to say, "Why are those two people talking to each other? What are they up to?"

If 3414 Peachtree is the Melrose Place of Atlanta's Private Banking scene, then Lenox Mall and Phipps Mall are the Barney's Greengrass: cool places to grab a coffee and gossip. We got our coffees and sat on a bench outside the mall.

Prior to my trip to Zurich I had asked him about the training program. Back then, he described his experience and how he lived it up during training. He was a bit of a wild man and I remember him telling me a story of a three-day weekend he had over Swiss Independence Day. The story ended with him saying, "All I'm saying is that after we threw the furniture off the balcony in our drunken stupor in Como, I'm probably never allowed back into Italy."

Back then, he laughed as he recalled his training escapades. Now as I sat next to him, it looked as though all happiness had been sucked out of his life. He looked different. Disillusioned.

He began our conversation by saying, "I'm going to tell you something that I wish someone would have told me."

It was like he was passing along insider information. Information that Eric Dale didn't want to tell us on those slides he gave us that said, "The Goals and Compensation for Associates on Teams." First thing he did was to break an unwritten rule among Associates. We never ever. Ever ever ever. Tell each other how much assets under management we have. It's super secretive and usually embarrassing because we have none.

He said, "I hit the $40 million dollar mark. I did it in December. My very last month I got a big account and made it to $40 million."

"That's great," I said. "Amazing. Congratulations. You're set."

The guy didn't even smile. He was a Private Banker with $40 million dollars under management and didn't even crack a smile.

"I'm going to tell you what happens in year three."

"Okay." He was like the ghost of what's yet to come.

"In year three you become a stockbroker."

"Wait. What? Say that again?"

"In year three you become a stockbroker."

He went on to describe what happened to him in December of 2010, the month before his salary ran out. This was a scene that I was nine months away from. In December of 2010, he was on the verge of opening a big account. It was an account that he always knew would come in, but he never knew when it would happen. Luckily, it happened in December or he would have been gone in January. In December, knowing that this big account was about to come in to get him up to the $40 million level that all of us were shooting for, he had a meeting with Major Major Cooper because his salary was going to run out in a couple of weeks.

Major Major Cooper said, "Don't worry we'll take care of you."

It was now the end of February and he had made exactly $0.00 for the year. His salary was cut off on January 1st and no one told him until January 13th. He was like the guy in the movie Office Space with the Swingline stapler. Major Major Cooper took care of him all right. He went back to Major Major and negotiated a draw down loan that would equate to about a $60,000 salary for the year that he would have to repay. Starting in mid-March he would get to draw on the loan at a max of $5,000 salary equivalent per month. Then, when the fees from his clients started to come in, the fees would be used to repay the loan. There were two other people in his class that were around the $40 million mark and they were given the loan deal as well.

"I haven't made any money this year," he said. "My wife has been paying for everything. She says I should quit. I don't know what I'm going to do. If I really get after it this year and get my assets up to $60 million, I'll still make less this year than I did last year. I lose money just coming into the office because I have to pay for parking. That big account that I got in December, now I'm trying to get the money invested as fast as possible because I need to get paid. Forget all that asset allocation stuff they teach you in training. You just want to get the money invested as fast as possible so you can get paid. In year three you become a stockbroker."

"Holy shit. You hit $40 million and now you make less?"

"Yeah. Those numbers that Eric Dale gives you are off."

I had my calculator, a notepad and a pencil and we ran the numbers. He gave me an example of a $14 million account he had. His whole team used Separately Managed Accounts. Here's how the money flows: First off, to win the $14 million dollar account they had to offer the client a blended yearly fee of 0.80%. Of that 0.80%, 0.40% goes to the Separately Managed Account managers and 0.40% goes to the firm. So, $56,000 goes to the firm. Of that $56,000, 65% is kept by the firm and 35% goes to the team which comes to $19,600. Those revenues are then split between the Associate and the team 50/50. On a $14 million account, the Associate makes $9,800 per year. If you take that same formula and apply it to $40 million in accounts, the Associate gets $28,000 per year. Now, let's just say that the team allows the Associate to keep all the revenues from the $40 million, then that's still only $56,000. Even if the Associate brings his assets up to $60 million, and the team lets him keep everything, then that is still only $84,000 per year. He was right. Even if he brought in another $20 million to get his assets up to $60 million he would still make less money unless the team took a cut in their own paychecks: not an easy sale. We thought that the numbers that Eric Dale was giving us were bad, but the fact of the matter was that the numbers were far worse.

The next couple of math problems we did were just for fun. We applied the same math to Jeremy Jones. It's very difficult to get Private Bankers to tell you exactly how much assets under management they have and how much their take home pay is but thanks to Goldman Sachs suing Jeremy Jones and *The Wall Street Journal* putting it on the front page, we had the numbers. Jeremy Jones's team had $1,400,000,000 under management. If he was using a blended Separately Managed Account rate of 0.80% and half of that was kept by the Separately Managed Account managers, then Jeremy Jones brought in $5,600,000 to the firm. Of that, $1,960,000 would go to the team. And, even though there were seven people on the team, only three weren't on salary. So, if you assume that among the three people off salary, Jeremy got 50% of the revenue and the other two got 25% of the revenue each, then Jeremy Jones would make $980,000 per year. Pretty damn close to the $1 million quoted by *The Wall Street Journal*. It was like doing a proof in high school algebra. The proof seemed to work.

We sat on the bench and did one more math problem. "How much do you think Credit Suisse paid for your $40 million?" I asked.

"What do you mean?" he asked.

"Well, if there were 11 people in your class and three had brought in about $40 million each, then how much did Credit Suisse pay in bonus and salary for the $120 million over two years?"

I used my Associate class as an example. From July 2009–February 2010 there were ten Associate in my class. Each of us got a $60,000 bonus and $63,333 in salary over those months. So, Credit Suisse paid $1,233,330.

From March 2010 to December 2010 there were nine Associates in my class and the firm paid us each $79,166.67 over that time. That's $712,500.

In January 2011, there were seven people left in my class and I assumed we would all work until the end of the year and collect our $95,000 salary. That's $665,000.

Credit Suisse paid my class $2,610,830 and if we did as good as the class before us we would bring in $120 million total. That $120 million would generate $480,000 in revenue for the firm. Credit Suisse was negative $2 million per Associate class. And, out of the three that made it to the $40 million mark, they were getting their salaries cut. How long would it take those three to pay back the firm the $2 million so that having an Associate class made sense? A long time. Maybe never.

"Well, if Credit Suisse is willing to pay a bunch of MBAs with more debt than contacts $2 million, then I guess paying Jeremy Jones $11 million doesn't sound like such a bad deal?" I said.

"That's what you have to shoot for. You have to get enough clients like Jeremy Jones and then leave. That's the way to do it," he said.

"Jeremy Jones is one hell of a salesman. You know his team of seven only brought in $89 million in 2010?"

"Really?"

"I sit right by Cooper's office." I smiled. "Apparently Goldman told all Jones's clients that all their fees would be waived for an entire year if they stayed. They're banking at Goldman for free. Why follow Jones to Credit Suisse? He doesn't have any investing talent. He just puts his clients in SMA accounts. Might as well stay at Goldman Sachs SMA accounts for free. I don't care how much bad press Goldman Sachs gets. It's still Goldman Sachs. Gonna be tough to get people to leave."

"It's the hardest job there is," he said.

We threw our coffee cups in a trash can and started to walk back to the office.

"What are you going to do?" I asked.

"I don't know. I've got a three thousand dollar mortgage. My wife has been paying for everything. I bet I could convince J.P Morgan or Goldman Sachs to put me back on salary and bring over a couple clients. I might do that. I haven't figured it out yet, but wanted to tell you what I wish someone would have told me. Oh yeah, and the new class of associates are getting paid $100,000. Apparently the MBAs are getting smarter."

Once I got back to my cube I couldn't think straight. I felt as though the wind had been knocked out of me. I looked over at Matlock's empty desk. Matlock missed 113 days in 2010. In the first two months of 2011 he worked 8 whole days. He never spoke to anyone. Never worked with anyone. Never opened any accounts. Yet, he was making more money than the guy with $40 million in assets.

The only way that paying $2.6 million for ten new Associate every year works is if one of those new Associates builds a billion dollar book of business to subsidize the guys like Matlock who do nothing. It was an expensive bet the firm was making. And, I wasn't even counting the trips to Zurich and expensive dinners and trips to New York and Summer associate internship salary. Credit Suisse pays millions of dollars for stockbrokers with no clients and more debt than contacts. All the firm had to do was stop hiring Matlocks and it would save millions. Then, take the money it saves on not hiring Matlocks and bonus the two or three that make it every year.

I thought the $2 million Credit Suisse pays stockbrokers with no clients was a lot, but Goldman Sachs has them beat. They hired about eighty new associates in Private Wealth Management in 2010. Their success rate is no better. So, they are losing about $16 million per year on stockbrokers with no clients. To prove my point, there are only five Private Bankers in Atlanta that have been with the firm more than five years, but they will hire eight new MBAs per year. Paying millions for stockbrokers with no clients makes no sense, but for some reason it has become "hot" on Wall Street.

CHAPTER THIRTY-ONE

The Ice Man Cometh

If you become a stockbroker in year three, then I had about nine months left before I hit the end of the ride. To snap myself out of my disillusionment, I wanted to throw myself into my work. I thought that was the best way to get out of the hopeless mindset that the meeting with the third year associate had put me in. I thought that I would enter a cold calling and cold emailing binge to help return to my blissful world where I collected a paycheck every two weeks and blast the thought of no money for months and a loan against commissions in January 2012. I already had student loans. Sallie Mae was a harsh mistress. The thought of any more loans in my life was unsettling.

Just before I went into cold call/cold email mode, something fantastic happened. I got an email from one of my old teammates from my Zurich training days. In fact, he was my best friend from training. He was there that night at Zur Oepfulchammer. We took our wives out together to a fun little pizza place in Shil City. We would drink wine and smoke cigarettes at Almodobar late at night after working on our Weissenstein presentation. He was there when University of Chicago girl threw up. And, he was onstage with me when we gave our Weissenstein presentation. In a short amount of time, we had become good buddies and in the business of geeks who can schmooze we both were more on the geek side of things. I'll name him LBS because that's where he went to school. London Business School.

LBS's email said that a case had just been referred to him regarding someone offshore that would like to open an account in the United States. LBS sent me the sample portfolio. $75 million.

It was an incredible stroke of luck. Just because I knew a guy in London I was going to get a chance to open a $75 million dollar account.

On the exact same day, four Credit Suisse Private Bankers were charged with conspiring to help US taxpayers hide up to $3 billion in assets. Their names were Maro Parenti Adami, Emanuel Agustoni, Michele Bergantino and Roger Schaerer. According to Matthew Barakat of the Associated Press, "the indictment claims the bankers discouraged customers from participating in a 2009 amnesty program offered by the Obama administration, in which U.S. taxpayers could avoid criminal prosecution if they came forward with information on their secret accounts and agreed to pay a penalty." Barakat wrote, "The Obama administration has been cracking down on foreign banks that it believes were helping U.S. taxpayers hide assets."

On the same day the Obama administration was going after Credit Suisse Private Bankers for taking money from the United States and hiding it offshore, I was a Credit Suisse Private Banker who was trying to take money from offshore and bring it to the United States. You're welcome, Obama.

***

Here's the thing. I got the $75 million client. I booked a flight to New York for a special meeting with the potential client. I got on the plane in Atlanta wearing a pair of jeans and a t-shirt and carrying a suit bag. I changed into my suit in a basement level bathroom of Eleven Madison Avenue like some sort of Superman-esque Private Banker and took the elevator up to the Private Banking floor. I held the meeting in a conference room right outside of Robert Weissenstin's (God's) office, then after the meeting took the elevator back down to the basement and put my jeans back on and booked it over to Torissi Italian Specialties for dinner at 6pm. After Torrisi I got back on a plane and flew back to Atlanta. It was one hell of a day trip.

After that first meeting, it took me months to close the deal. Calls with the client. Calls with New York. Web-Ex presentations. Tons of follow-up calls and meetings and negotiating of fees. Marathon email chains. I ran the whole process myself and in the end I won the account. It was one of the most complex deals I've ever been a part of and when I got it I became the top Private Banker in my entire Associate Class: bringing in more assets to the firm than anyone else. You will never guess who brought in the second most assets. It was University of Chicago Girl. Yes, the same girl that didn't know what a derivative was, didn't pass her Series 66 on the first try, and fell in her own vomit during our Zurich case presentation. None of that mattered because her family knew people. And, I have to tell you that I was overjoyed that I surpassed her. She had $45 million in assets. The next closest was $30 million (his biggest account was because of his family too). And, the rest of the class was doomed.

But here's the rub. Due to the way the fees are calculated and because Mr. Big wasn't doing any investing at the moment, my reward for bringing in $75 million would be total compensation in 2012 of $26,687.5. The total fees that this new account would generate every year for the firm are $152,500.

The firm would keep 65% of those fees. After Credit Suisse took its cut, there would be $53,375 left. Of that $53,375, I would have to give half to the Private Banker offshore who referred the client but didn't actually do any work on the account. That Private Banker offshore would get half for the first two years. After the offshore Private Banker got his cut, there would be $26,687.5 left over for me. Assuming that Alex would let me keep all of that and not make me split some with him then I would make $26,687.5 in 2012. If Alex took a split, then I was really screwed.

After taxes, that would be enough money to make the minimum payments on my Student Loans and almost pay my rent.

My reward was adjusted gross income in 2012 that would be considered just about poverty. New Associates just out of MBA with no clients were getting hired for $100,000 per year and I just brought in $75 million and my income was going to be slashed to $26,678.5.

As these thoughts were running through my mind I went online and found a clip of Michael Lewis speaking to a group of students. I was looking for a friend to help me through a tough time in my career and thought just maybe Michael Lewis would be the one. In the clip, he said, "write what you know." I watched the clip over and over and over. That same weekend I attended an event at my alma mater Emory University featuring Salman Rushdie speaking about writing a memoire. After that event I went back home and pulled up the Michael Lewis clip for what was nowhere near the first or last time. I had followed in Michael Lewis's footsteps by doing Asset Securitization. Why not follow in his footsteps again?

For the next month I wrote my face off. I wrote while I was at work. I wrote at nights at home and on the weekends. I listened to indie rock and started smoking cigarettes while writing. That was my image of cool writers and I thought to myself, "why not?" I even tried waking up early and writing while drinking coffee and smoking cigarettes. I thought cigarettes in the morning were disgusting so I suppose I'm not very cool. I put my butt in the chair, bought some smokes to smoke at night with bourbon, or as my wife referred to my drink of choice that month "Roses and Coke," and wrote and watched *Wall Street* movies. As other writers before me have discovered, whiskey and cigarettes proved to be fuel for the empty page. I would write at work and print out pages on the office printer and shove them into my pockets and walk out of the office at night feeling like the Shawshank Redemption: substitute rocks for folded up pieces of paper.

I did research at the Emory library and searched around to see if any other Private Banker had written anything other than the typical sales 101 stuff by some guy that I would definitely like to punch in the face. There was nothing out there. The only inspiration I had was the Michael Lewis clip. I had been influenced by him before and took a job in Asset Securitization. Now, I would try to write a book. Everything that you just read is what I did in that smoke-filled month. At that point, it seemed more feasible that I would be able to write a book than to make a living at Credit Suisse in 2012 after my salary ran out. So I did it.

My wife thought I was just going through a phase or doing a boy project, but what she didn't know was that there was a major piece to my story that I needed to resolve. Credit Suisse was about to be done with me, but I wasn't done with it. I wanted to go to Dubai, London and Zurich. I wanted to find out what the hell happened to everyone else.

I wanted to find out how Wealth Management worked in the rest of the world. Was everyone experiencing what I was going through? Was everyone turning into a stockbroker in year three? Or, did other countries treat Wealth Management differently? I needed to reconnect with my fellow Associates from around the world and find out. How much money do they make? What is their job like? What's their story?

And, more than anything in the whole world, I wanted to successfully complete the Zur Oephelchammer challenge. But what might prove to be even harder than the Zur Oephelchammer challenge is the Mrs. Kidd challenge: convincing my wife that after not succeeding at my job that seemed so amazing at graduation, I needed to traipse all over the world and have fun.

PART II:

END OF THE JOB

CHAPTER THIRTY-TWO

Forty Million Dollars, The Kids Don't Stand A Chance

In case you haven't noticed, I like indie rock music. I've referenced it and I've also hidden some lyrics in my writing, but I'm going to be absolutely blatant about the title to this chapter.

I've racked my brain over music lyrics that might describe my two years of Private Banking better than those lyrics written by Ezra Koenig of Vampire Weekend and I can't think of any better. When I think back on my Associate Class meeting with Eric Dale, back when all of us were still in training and still had jobs at the bank, I like to imagine this song played over the scene of us being told we had two years to bring in forty million dollars. I imagine us scribbling in our notebooks and some of us naively nodding our heads with Ezra Koenig crooning "Forty Million Dollars, The kids don't stand a chance" playing over the scene of us in our pin-striped suits that morning in the One Madison office of Credit Suisse with the view of the New York skyline behind us.

Now, I had brought in a $75 million account and my income was going to get slashed. I just couldn't wrap my mind around it. I did my job. I stepped up to the challenge under immense pressure. I brought in more assets than anyone in my Associate class, but I was going to get my income cut. I had a feeling that if I worked as a Private Banker in any other country, I would be rewarded.

In the May 28-29, 2011 Weekend Edition of *The* Wall Street Journal, Ian Salisbury wrote the following in an article entitled, "Investors Get Better Tools To Price Financial Advisors."

"Once pegged "stockbrokers" who primarily peddled securities for Wall Street firms, the nation's financial advisors have been slowly transforming themselves over the past decade into a new class of professional that aims to counsel investors on how to save, spend, and invest."

My thought was that the rest of the world had already made this transition and done it effectively and that the United States' financial advisors were nothing more than stockbrokers in financial advisors' clothing. I had a feeling that the United States was still in the Dark Ages when it came to wealth management.

To find out how the rest of the world treated Private Banking and Wealth Management, I would go on a walkabout. I would take a week off of my job and seek the truth. The idea of an adventure that would lead me to Dubai, London and Zurich made me think of Chris McCandless going Into The Wild. I've always sort of felt a connection to McCandless. We both went to the same college. We both love reading Wendell Barry, Wallace Stegner and Thoreau. Yes, we are 100% different in our outlook on life, but there had to be something similar inside us to draw us to those authors. Like McCandless, I like to quote Stegner. I've even met Wendell Barry. And, I would have to say that Thoreau's views on home mortgages are about the same as my own views on student loans. Another connection I have to McCandless is that the first time I ever laid eyes on the girl that would become my wife, she was standing right next to Emile Hirsch who was fresh off of filming Into The Wild. Hirsch was there looking like McCandless: Bearded. Skinny. Homeless. It was as if McCandless was there, at the party where I met my wife. Because of all these things, I've always felt a little connection to McCandless. And, I think it was with a similar spirit that I wanted to go on a walkabout. I needed adventure and truth.

Don't get me wrong though, McCandless and I are extremely different. Unlike McCandless, I didn't have college paid for me and I wasn't given $47,000 for my graduate education. When it comes to money, that's where we differ. I've had student loans since the day I first set foot on a campus back in 1995 and I'm sick of them. McCandless might have donated his grad school money to charity, but I would work my butt off for years just to pay back my loans. In this vain, I'm more like Bud Fox. To quote Bud talking to his dad about borrowing money, "I've got student loans." Bud had his dad would argue over student loans more than once. Yeah, I hear you, Bud.

I was a young American about to go on walkabout. I set some ground rules and structure. I would give myself one week. I would buy the cheapest plane ticket possible and stay in the cheapest hotel rooms I could find on Orbitz. In Dubai, I would meet with Oxford Dubai. In London, I would meet with London City. In Zurich, I would meet with Russian Girl. After all of my meetings, I would finish my walkabout with a physical challenge: the jump at Zur Oepfulchammer. I thought that I needed something to symbolize the end of my job. A good challenge that would allow me to say okay, I'm done. This is the end. I needed a physical challenge that could instill a change in me and provide closure.

The first thing I did was to do a quick search on Orbitz to see how much this thing was going to set me back. If it was really expensive, I probably couldn't swing it. I went online and picked a week as my test itinerary. I would leave on a Thursday and return on a Thursday. In between I would hit all the countries I wanted to hit. I typed everything into Orbitz and clicked "Find." As the Orbitz screen ticked off time processing my request, I kept saying to myself, "Please don't cost a million dollars. Please don't cost a million dollars." After a few seconds, the price and itinerary appeared. $1,326. Not bad. And, Atlanta to Dubai was a direct flight, which was a nice bonus. Everything else had a layover in Paris. Considering my in-direct flight to Zurich two years prior was about $2,000, I thought this was a good deal.

I also did a search to confirm that the exact itinerary worked for the week prior, just to give myself some flexibility in scheduling meetings. Sure the itinerary worked, but could I actually fit myself into everyone's busy schedules in one week's time in three different countries? I sent out emails in the order of the itinerary.

Me: Do you want to meet for coffee, drink or dinner on Saturday, May 14 or 21st? I'm planning a trip and thought it might be fun to catch up. Let me know if you'll be around.

Oxford Dubai: Dear W.E., Good to hear from you. I would be happy to meet up for a coffee on 21st of May since I am traveling on the previous dates. Please give me a call on xxx-xxx-xxx once you are in Dubai and we can coordinate. Hope all is well. Cheers!

Me: That's fantastic. I'll send you an email that week just as a reminder and I'll give you a call on the 21st. Looking forward to it!

Notice how I intentionally kept my reason for coming to Dubai vague. I didn't know what the heck to say, so I didn't say anything. I would figure it out when we met up because it would eventually come up, right? *Uhhh…so what exactly are you doing here all by yourself?*

The good news was that setting the meeting was incredibly easy. Almost too easy. So, next I went on to email London City.

Me: I'm planning a trip to London and want to see if you would like to grab a pint or lunch on May 22nd or 23rd. I could also do an early morning coffee on the 24th if that works. Let me know if you are around, it would be great to catch up.

London City: Would love to. I can do any of those days. Why don't you come over to my

place for lunch on the 22nd? We can have an
English style Sunday Lunch with all the
trimmings. Also, I have resigned from Credit
Suisse starting in a couple of weeks, so
might want to use my home e-mail for future
contact.

Me: An English style lunch sounds fantastic! Sorry to hear about resigning, but I look forward to catching up. I can tell you all about the rest of the class from the US. I'll use your home e-mail going forward and will send you an e-mail the week before the 22nd to confirm. And, I think I have your mobile. Looking forward to it.

Notice how different London City is from Oxford Dubai. Oxford Dubai only had time for a coffee. London City, the most English person I've ever met, invites me over to his house for none other than an English style Sunday lunch with all the trimmings. I honestly couldn't wait. I've never had all of the trimmings before. I don't even know if I've ever had *some* of the trimmings. I was so curious as to what these trimmings were going to consist of. Needless to say, London City is a fantastic person. I might have liked to poke fun at how incredibly British he was in training, but he just invited me over to his house for lunch. I was honored. Not only that, when I had needed to get some information from him for a client of Alex's that was moving to the UK and needed financing, London City knew everything. He's a good banker and a great person. Setting meetings with Oxford Dubai and London City was easy. Now, I just had to set my meeting with Russian Girl in Zurich.

Me: I'm going to be passing through town with some friends on May 25th and 26th. I can do a coffee or lunch on the 25th

or early morning coffee on the 26th. Will you be around? It would be fun to catch up. I can tell you all about the rest of the class.

Russian Girl: Hey Welcome!! Sure, so far both dates look open. I think lunch would work on the 25th. Let me know.

Me: Great. Let's set it for lunch on the 25th. Name a time and place that work for you and I'll see you there.

Russian Girl: Yes, perfect. Where do you think you will be in Zurich? Center? What do you want to eat?

Me: I'll be in the center, but can meet wherever. As for eating, I like anything. If you pick somewhere you like that will work for me.

Russian Girl: So, Let's meet at 11:30 at Rennweg tram stop in front of the Coop (it is the grocery store). Then we can go from there. We can do earlier lunch, because things get really busy at 12. Let me know if that works.

Me: Perfect. I'll shoot you an email the day before to confirm. Looking forward to it.

The Rennweg tram stop is on Bahnhofstrasse right where the book *The Numbered Account* begins. If my grandma only knew how appropriate that book would become for me when she gave it to me back in 1996. I couldn't believe my life had taken such a turn that I was now setting up secret meetings off of Bahnhofstrasse with a Russian Swiss Banker. But I needed the adventure and truth. I needed to find out how the rest of the world's wealth managers work. With the confirmation of the meeting with Russian Girl, my schedule had been set. I felt a little bad about telling Russian Girl that I was going to be "passing through with some friends." But I couldn't say that I was trying to write a book. I had to lie.

The Last piece of planning was making my hotel reservations. I restricted myself to not paying more than $100 per night including tax. This was a far cry from the $500 per night hotel I stayed at in Zurich during training. I went back to Orbitz and did some searching.

Including tax, my week's worth of lodging would be $435.34. Travel and lodging for the entire trip would equal $1,761.34. After scheduling everything, I had about a month to train and worry.

Scheduling everything was easy compared to the Zur Oepfulhammer challenge, the last piece of my walkabout. To prepare for the challenge, I began a regimen of upper body and lower body work-outs: squats, lunges, jumping over a stack of Reebok steps, pull-ups, chin-ups, push-ups, standing row, and pull-downs. Four times a week during my lunch hour, I would go down to the gym in our building and workout. I even bought a new pair of shoes to help with the vertical leap: a pair of Nike Zoom Waffle Racer VII Track and Field shoes. They were red with grey webbing and looked like something Peter Parker would wear. They were extremely light. Wearing them, I felt like I was wearing nothing at all. I also called Zur Oepfulchammer to make sure they would be open when I was in Zurich, which they would be.

That month seemed to take forever to pass. I would wake up mornings full of confidence and go to bed at night scared as hell that I was making a big mistake. Worried about not making any money in 2012. Worried that I was going to fail my walkabout. Worried that I was going to get in trouble for trying to write a book. Worried that customs agents would stop me at the airport because I was a Swiss Banker doing something suspicious. According to the April 8th 2009 edition of *The Wall Street Journal,* Swiss Bankers had to be careful about travel. Here's a blurb from the article entitled, "Crackdown shackles Swiss Private Bankers.":

"Swiss private bankers are becoming wary about travelling abroad, underscoring how hard a global crackdown on tax avoidance is hitting the discreet business of providing banking services to the wealthy. UBS AG, the world's largest manager of private wealth by assets, had barred "client-facing" staff in its wealth-management divisions from traveling abroad–a move aimed at avoiding further trouble for the bank, which already has had two bankers arrested as part of a continuing U.S. investigation into tax fraud."

I would lie awake at night imagining customs agents looking at the Suisse work Visa stamp in my passport from two years prior, see my profession listed as banker, look at my itinerary to Dubai, London and Zurich, then without any questioning haul me off to jail because I could only be up to no good.

I would lie awake at night asking myself, "What in the world are you thinking? Are you writing an expose? I'm sure your Swiss Bank employer known for its banking secrecy is going to love you using real numbers." The only thing that helped me keep my sanity was the clip of Michael Lewis. I would watch it over and over.

CHAPTER THIRTY-THREE

Where Have All Of The Stockbrokers Gone – Part III

To prepare for my walkabout and investigation into how Private Banking works outside of the United States, I did some more research on Private Banking and Wealth Management vs. Stockbrokers. Since I was going to the United Arab Emirates, the United Kingdom and Switzerland, I wanted to know how popular the terms "Private Banking," "Wealth Management" and "Stockbroker" were in those countries. Luckily for me each country had a lot of English language publications.

I conducted the same Factiva search that I did on a global scale, but now I confined my search to only the countries I would be visiting. Here's what I found when searching English-only publications in the United Arab Emirates:

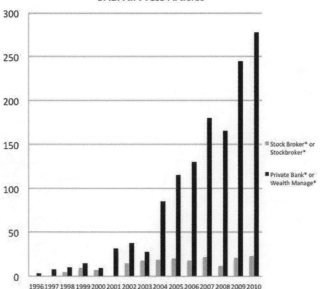

The data that I found for the UAE was similar to what I found on a global scale. The term stockbroker is hardly ever used, and the terms Private Banking and Wealth Management have become increasingly popular and have risen out of nothing starting in around 1996. This led me to believe that when I got to Dubai, I would be in a city where the Stockbroker didn't exist. The data said to me that a more holistic approach to Wealth Management was in place in Dubai since Dubai had no stock market and boomed in a time when the terms Private Bank and Wealth Management were becoming en vogue.

Next, I did the same search for the United Kingdom. Here are the results:

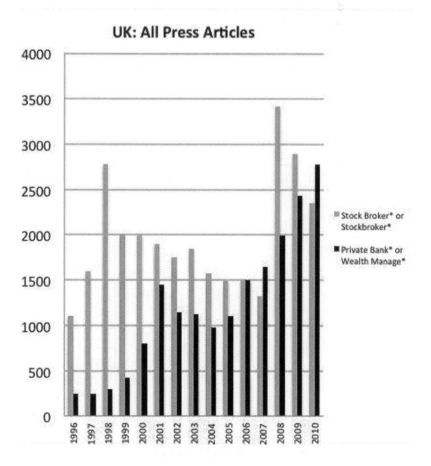

In the United Kingdom, it appeared that the Stockbroker was alive and well. I couldn't believe it. The United Kingdom was completely different than what I expected. Almost every year that I searched, the term stockbroker was more popular than the terms Private Bank or Wealth Management combined. At first I thought maybe Stockbroker means something different in the United Kingdom. After all, the English term for soccer is football. The English term for bachelor party is stag doo. Maybe in the United Kingdom stockbroker meant cattle farmer or something like that. Could the stockbroker really be alive in England? To find out, I went to a UK job search site and searched for "stockbroker" jobs. Four pages of jobs appeared. Stockbrokers really did exist in the UK. I couldn't wait to get there and find out exactly how they differed from Private Bankers.

To test out my theory that in the United States Private Bankers are really just stockbrokers in Financial Advisors clothing, I went to the US job site careerbuilder.com and searched for "stockbroker" jobs. Five pages of jobs for "financial advisor" came up. For some reason, the stockbroker term died in the United States but was alive and well in the United Kingdom.

Finally, I searched Switzerland's English-only publications. Here are the results:

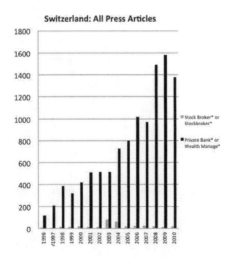

The results for Switzerland were not surprising. Switzerland is the home of Private Banking and bank secrecy. It's no surprise that the terms Private Bank and Wealth Management are used more often.

What all this research said to me was that England was making the transition from stockbrokers that peddled securities to financial advisors counseling investors on a wide range of services, similar to the United States. However, Switzerland and the United Arab Emirates had never even bothered with stockbrokers and went straight to financial advisors. There was really no transition for them. Did the fact that the United States and England have some of the biggest stock exchanges in the world affect the job of the personal financial advisor? More importantly, did it affect how I was getting paid? And, did it affect the size of Jeremy Jones's signing bonus?

Since my whole theory was that the United States was full of stockbrokers in Private Banker's clothing and the rest of the world was more advanced, I did one last search. I thought it would be fun to find a career guide from 1997, the year Jeremy Jones started his job at Goldman Sachs, and see if anything had changed.

After a little searching, I found a book called "Careers For The Year 2000 And Beyond." It was published in 1997 by Research and Education and Association. Here's a description of a "securities sales representative" a.k.a. stockbroker from 1997:

Nature of the Work

"The most important part of a sales representative's job is finding clients and building a customer base. Thus, beginning securities sales representatives spend much of their time searching for customers – relying heavily on telephone solicitation. They may meet some clients through business and social contacts. Many sales representatives find it useful to get additional exposure by teaching adult education investment courses or by giving lectures at libraries or social clubs. Brokerage firms may give sales representatives lists of people with whom the firm has done business with in the past. Sometimes sales representatives may inherit the clients of representatives who have retired."

Job Outlook

"Due to the highly competitive nature of securities sales work, many beginners leave the field because they are unable to establish a sufficient clientele."

This described my job exactly. I was a securities sales rep! Why the fuck didn't they put that on the job description for Private Banker. I'll tell you why. No MBA would do it. Here's what the earnings were out of a book published the same year Jeremy Jones started.

Earnings

"In 1994, median annual earnings of securities and financial services sales representatives were $37,300. Ten percent earned less than $17,600. Ten percent earned more than $120,700.

Trainees are usually paid a salary until they meet licensing and registration requirements. After candidates are licensed and registered their earnings depend on commissions from the sale or purchase of stock and bonds, life insurance, or other securities for customers."

This was my job! Private Bankers in the United States are really just Securities Sales Representatives except now trainees get $60,000 signing bonus and $100,000 for two years. Trainees who are stockbrokers with no clients make good money. And Jeremy Jones gets $11 million signing bonus and doesn't even have to bring over all his clients. Nowhere in the earnings description did it mention million dollar signing bonuses. When Jeremy Jones took his job at Goldman Sachs in 1997 it would have been unimaginable for him to think if the stock market was at about the same place thirteen years from now, I will garner an $11 million bonus for switching firms. Fortunately for him, the mystique of the stockbroker changed and he sold at the top.

The description of the job is the exact same. But for some reason it has become hot on Wall Street because instead of calling it Stockbroker or Securities Sales Representative it is now called Private and has a mystique. But if you read the description, it's the same. And, in year three you really do become a stockbroker. My theory was that the rest of the world is different. And, I was about to find out if I was right.

CHAPTER THIRTY-FOUR

Bud and I Go To Dubai

Here is what was going through my mind as my wife drove me to the airport for my flight to Dubai, "There's a huge fucking difference between saying you're going to do something and doing it. Doing it is scary as hell. There are about 50 million ways this trip could end in utter failure, jail, physical harm, you name it." I was extremely worried and felt like I was a crazy person making a mistake. I couldn't believe my wife could look at me and not think I was crazy. She could see the worry in my eyes and as we took the exit for the airport she said to me, "Sometimes you have to do crazy things and take big risks to get what you are looking for."

In hindsight, it was the perfect thing to say, but at the time it didn't work. It didn't calm me down. I felt like I had just dreamed up this crazy thing to do and now that I was actually doing it it seemed even crazier. I didn't tell my wife this, but one of the biggest worries I had was that Oxford Dubai had cancelled on me. That's right. I was going to Dubai and had no confirmed meeting. This was not supposed to be a vacation. This was supposed to be a mission and the first part of the mission just got screwed up.

Earlier in the week, I emailed Oxford Dubai to confirm the meeting.

Me: Just want to confirm coffee on Saturday the 21st. I looked up a place called Lime Tree Café. Is that a good place to meet? Let me know a time and place that work for you and I'll meet you there.

Oxford Dubai: Good morning, I regret to inform you that I will not be able to meet you on Saturday. I am traveling for work at the moment and am currently in London. I will be back only mid next week. I apologize for the late response and would have loved to meet with you if I was around. If you are here on holiday please let me know if you need anything and I will be happy to help. Hope all is well. I hope we will have another chance to meet soon in Dubai or the States.

I got that email the day before I was to get on the plane. If Oxford Dubai ever reads this I would like to give him some advice. Don't ever start an email with the words, "Good morning, I regret to inform you." It makes it seem like you are about to tell me someone died. In this case, I suppose it was me that died. I was dead because now I had no meeting and no purpose for flying all the way to the Middle East. I was so screwed. What if everyone else cancelled on me? The trip could easily turn into me just hopping around from country to country without a purpose. I emailed Oxford Dubai back. Maybe I could meet with him in London. I was going to be there at the same time as him. Maybe I could still find out how Private Banking works in Dubai even if I wasn't in Dubai when I found out.

Me: This could actually still work. I'm in London from Sunday–Tuesday morning. LBS and I are meeting up for dinner on Monday night if you want to join us. Or, we could just grab a drink on Sunday night or Monday night. I've also got Monday morning open for a coffee if that works. Let me know what works for you.

Oxford Dubai: I am embarrassed to say that I am unable to meet in London as well, I have a very tight schedule and am travelling across England in my trip with only a few days in London city. I will not be able to confirm in advance and it is not fair to give you a tentative time. Please accept my apologies for this time and I promise to catch up with you the next time I am in Atlanta. Hope this is ok. Cheers!

Fuck. That's how I felt about that. Now I was an idiot flying to Dubai for absolutely no reason whatsoever. It was the day before my flight and I had to figure out a new plan. He was the only person in my Associate training class that was to start in the Dubai office, but I had heard that someone from my Associate class who started in the Geneva office had moved to the Dubai office. I'll call him INSEAD Dubai. I went on the corporate intranet and found him. Sure enough, INSEAD Dubai was no longer working out of the Geneva office. He *was* in Dubai! I emailed him:

Me: I'm going to be passing through Dubai on Friday night and Saturday. Will you be around? Do you have time for a coffee or bite to eat or something?

I sent that the night before my trip and didn't get a response until the morning of my trip.

INSEAD Dubai: Yes let's try to catch up. My weekend is pretty busy but should be able to make time. Just let me know what times

exactly you arrive and leave and where you
are staying, and I'll suggest something.

I didn't like how he used the words "let's try" and "should be able to." I wanted a definite meeting, but this was much better than nothing.

Me: I arrive at 7:40 pm on Friday and leave around midnight on Saturday. I'm staying near the world trade center but can meet anywhere that works for you. I don't have any plans. This is just a one day layover for me, but it should be fun because I've never been to Dubai.

That is how I left it as my wife was dropping me off at the airport. I had no confirmed meeting. My wife and I kissed at curbside Delta check-in and I walked away with my backpack and small red suitcase in tow. I took my first step on my walkabout and still felt worried because everything wasn't going according to plan.

I checked in and as I was going through customs, the customs agent looked at me, looked at my passport and asked where I was going. I said, "Dubai," half expecting to get hauled off as a suspect for helping wealthy people avoid paying taxes.

The customs agent looked up from my passport and said, "Keep an open mind, man. Just roll with it."

I don't know why he said it, but it made me feel better. Sometimes unexpected words from strangers work. Why in the world did he say that to me? Did he know I was going on a walkabout? I'll never know, but I was starting to feel more confident about the trip. It was as if he told me exactly what I needed to hear.

I walked around the International terminal, bought a Universal adapter and exchanged some dollars for dirham. Boarding the plane went smoothly and as we were about to pull away from the gate, I reached into my pocket to turn off my Blackberry and noticed that my wife just sent me a text:

Margaret: Just opened a Magic Hat – the cap says "be a traveler, not a tourist" thought it could be good advice for you. Miss you, have a good flight xoxo

Magic Hat is a great beer from Vermont that has words of wisdom printed underneath the bottle cap. That's how cool my wife is. She drinks Magic Hat beer alone and reads the caps.

Me: wow…perfect. Thanks honey. Got voice, text and email enabled. Text is very cheap. Love you.

This is how my brain works. I can't not mention when I get something "cheap."

Margaret: Perfect. Love you love you love you.

Finally, between my wife, the customs agent and the Magic Hat bottle cap, I felt like maybe I was doing the right thing. I turned my Blackberry off and settled in for the 13hr and 26 minute flight, which would take me from the busiest airport in the world to the biggest airport in the world.

Once the plane had taken off and reached a safe altitude, I pulled up the list of movies that were available to me. These days, the list is quite extensive. Scrolling through the list, I came across a film that I was not expecting to find: *Wall Street*.

About five seconds later, Frank Sinatra was singing "Fly Me to the Moon," set to the beautiful backdrop of 1980's New York City.

When you've watched the movie *Wall Street* as many times as me, you start to pick up on the little things. This viewing of the film on my tiny screen was no different. On this viewing, the beginning of my walkabout, I really keyed in on the scene that is set to The Talking Heads song "This Must Be The Place." It's the scene where Bud is first starting to make it. He buys an apartment on the Upper East Side and cooks a fancy meal with his girlfriend Darien. The thing that occurred to me on this viewing that I had never noticed before is that this dinner that I've thought of my whole life as being fancy is nothing more than spaghetti marinara with a side of sushi. Gross. I had never paid attention before as to what was on their plates. They make such a big deal about how fantastic it is, but it's just spaghetti with a side of sushi. I can forgive all of the bad women's clothes and interior decorating of the 80's. Stylistic tastes change. But taste buds don't change. Spaghetti and sushi don't mix. Maybe Oliver Stone had some sort of weird craving late at night while writing and it worked its way into the movie.

Another thing I noticed is that during that scene, one of the lines from the Talking Heads song is "never for money always for love." Has anyone else ever noticed this? In the movie that is famous for Gordon Gekko saying, "Greed is Good," you also have David Byrne of the Talking Heads belting out, "never for money always for love." I don't think it's a coincidence.

Regardless of my obsessive intimate knowledge of the movie, watching *Wall Street* was the perfect way to begin the walkabout. It is my favorite movie. And, the Talking Heads "This Must Be

The Place," had just become my current favorite song. It was perfect.

Bud and I were going to Dubai together.

CHAPTER THIRTY-FIVE

Dubai

The plane landed and I arrived safely after watching *Wall Street* , *Wall Street II* and a couple of other movies. I looked around the plane and thought to myself, "Man, what are you doing here?" After the flight attendant announced that we could use electronic devices, I powered on my Blackberry and read the following message:

INSEAD Dubai: How about breakfast at 9 on Saturday morning? Which hotel are you in? We could just meet there, or I'll pick you up and we can go somewhere nearby. My number in Dubai is xxx xxxxxx. Feel free to call.

My journey had taken a turn for the better. Now, I knew what I was there for. It was 7:40 p.m. GST and I had a purpose. I was going to save money on cab fare, too. Bonus. I replied back:

Me: Just landed. That sounds great! I'm at the Ibis World Trade Center. Thanks INSEAD Dubai…looking forward to it. I'll give you a call around 8:30 tomorrow morning just to confirm. And my cell is xxx-xxx-xxxx.

I could have gone out on the town that night and gone to a club or a hip restaurant or taken in the sights, but I didn't. I wasn't a tourist. I was a traveler. I checked into my room, bought a pack of Marlboro Lights to smoke while sitting on a bench outside my hotel watching people go to and fro from a dance club. I thought about what I wanted to find out in my meeting the next morning. I knew I wanted to cover a few big things such as how much money you make in Dubai, how does Private Banking work in the UAE, and do you like it? I went to bed early that night because I wanted to be fresh in the morning.

***

Credit Suisse Dubai is located in the Dubai International Financial Center or "DIFC." The DIFC is a financial free zone established by Sheik Mohammed bin Rashid Maktoum in 2004. It is 110-acre plot of land in the heart of the city. Firms registered in the DIFC are independent of the laws of the UAE because the DIFC has its own civil and commercial laws. The opening of the DIFC in 2004 drew all the big banks to the UAE: Goldman Sachs, Citi, Deutsche, Credit Suisse, UBS, JP Morgan, Morgan Stanley, Barclays, HSBC, BNP Paribas. You get the idea. If you are a Private Banker in the UAE, chances are your office is in the DIFC.

The Credit Suisse office is in a building called The Gate, which is one of the most popular buildings in all of Dubai. With all of the new incredible buildings, that's saying something. The Gate was designed by Gensler, one of the biggest architectural firms in the United States. Gensler designed the building to be modeled after the Arc de Triumph in Paris as a way of symbolizing it as the gateway to Dubai's new financial center. Gensler describes The Gate as embodying the DIFC's values of integrity, transparency, and simplicity. Personally, I think it looks like a Borg cube from Star Trek.

INSEAD Dubai picked me up from my hotel early Saturday morning and we drove over to The Gate. It had been about two years since we last saw each other, but it felt like no time had passed. During training, we didn't have a lot in common: just two guys from separate countries trying to impress senior management.

But now we had been doing the same job for two years and had war stories to swap and insights to share. I could tell he was just as excited to talk about what his job was like as I was to tell him about what it was like in the United States.

Inside the Gate there is a restaurant called More. *Time Out Magazine* has called it one of the best café's in Dubai and made special mention of its breakfasts. I was glad INSEAD Dubai picked it. We both ordered Eggs Benedict and then INSEAD Dubai went into his story.

He began his Private Banking career in Geneva. His salary was $120,000 Swiss Francs. At the time of our breakfast, this was equivalent to about $142,000 American dollars. In addition to the $142,000 he also got what he described as a very nice bonus. So, I'm guessing that his total compensation was around $200,000.

INSEAD Dubai's job title was the exact same as mine, except his job was much different. As he described it, he was much more of a secretary supporting a team of Private Bankers. It was demoralizing. He had just gotten his MBA. He was an engineer before getting his MBA. Then, he studied finance for two years at INSEAD. And his new job was basically secretarial work. Filing papers. Making copies. There was no client interaction, but the beauty of it was that he would be on salary and bonus forever. His salary wouldn't be cut to zero after 24 months like it is for Private Bankers in the United States. It might have been demoralizing, but at least he was getting paid and getting paid well. He was making about $200,000 and never had to find new clients for the firm.

He was satisfied with the money, but wasn't satisfied with the job. Plus, he didn't like working in Geneva. Some might romanticize about being a Private Banker in Switzerland, but the story INSEAD Dubai was telling wasn't romantic at all. His apartment was small and expensive. He had a hard time making friends with other people in Geneva because he wasn't from there and didn't ski. And his wife, who also wasn't from there, wanted to leave.

INSEAD Dubai's intent was always to leave the Geneva office and move to the Dubai office. Prior to business school, both he and his wife had been living in Dubai. His wife got pregnant and wanted to have the baby in Dubai with an English speaking doctor. He leveraged this to move to a Private Banking team in Dubai and after about a year and a half in Geneva, he made the move.

Once he got to Dubai, his life and job changed for the better. First of all, he was paid even more money plus a bonus. So now, he has got to be over $200,000. As opposed to the small apartment he had in Geneva, he now has a four bedroom villa. And he is a proud father.

His Private Banking title is the same, but his team in Dubai doesn't use him as a secretary. They gave him his own accounts. When he said this I about fell out of my chair. I stopped him at this point in his story.

"Wait. You get a salary and bonus. You get your salary and bonus forever. And, you were given accounts?"

"Yeah. When I tell other people in Dubai and Switzerland about you Americans and commission only, they can't believe it. However, the accounts I was given were accounts that other people didn't really want. They are problem accounts."

I really didn't feel sorry for him and his problem accounts. He had a guaranteed salary and had been given clients. Problems or no problems. His job sounded great.

"Do you cold call?"

"No. I should. I spent my first six months working on the accounts that were given to me and I've been following up on a lot of team referrals."

He doesn't cold call and he never once mentioned having to use his dad or his family to get clients. His Private Banking job was amazing. His team gave him their referrals! Why was it so different ? I suppose one reason is that if you are on salary and bonus, you don't care too much if you help younger guys on your team get some accounts – chances are your salary and bonus will still be pretty good. But, in the United States, if you give a client to a new person on your team then that is money out of your pocket. In the U S, the commissions each client generates is carved up so that goes directly to the broker. And, it's carved up so much that it is very difficult to bring in enough to support yourself if you are just starting out. I was jealous of INSEAD Dubai with his salary and accounts given to him.

He went on to describe his team. The Private Banking office in Dubai covers India, Africa and the Middle East. INSEAD Dubai's team covers the Gulf Coast Countries or "GCC" which consists of Saudi Arabia, Kingdom of Bahrain, Kuwait, Qatar, and Oman. There were about fifteen members of his team in total, all covering these countries. They all worked together. This was so different than my office of twenty-eight, carved into six different teams, all competing against each other. We had six teams competing against each other to cover Atlanta. They had one team covering four countries!

After he was done with his story, he said to me, "I'm still hungry. Want to split some pancakes?"

It was at that moment that INSEAD Dubai and I became friends because it is impossible to split pancakes with someone who isn't your friend. And, anyone that knows me knows I love pancakes. We ordered some Dutch pancakes, Pannekoeken, and they were delicious.

I asked if there was such a thing as $11 million dollar signing bonuses in Dubai even if you didn't bring over all of your clients.

"No. I've never heard of anything like that."

Amazing. So far, Jeremy Jones deals only existed in the United States. I told INSEAD Dubai about the rest of the class. I told him that 40% was wiped out so far. Everyone was worried about what happens in January. Will they be able to pay their mortgage? Will they be able to support their kids? I told him that I had just brought in $75 million.

"$75 million. That's incredible. Congratulations! You're set," he said.

Then I told him that it means about $26,000 in salary. Probably about 1/10th what he was making.

"Oh. That sucks."

"If I brought in $75 million in Dubai, would that be good?"

"Yeah. That would be a good year. You wouldn't get fired that's for sure. So what are you going to do?"

"I don't know."

That was a lie and I felt bad lying to my new pancake friend. At this point I obviously knew I was leaving the firm. I was going all Michael Lewis on the firm. But I couldn't say that. I couldn't. What I did tell him was like all lies, something that contains a little truth. I told him that I had a layover in Dubai on my way to England for the last English Premiership match of the season. I was going to go see Arsenal vs. Fulham and the plane ticket was much cheaper for some crazy reason if I had a layover in Dubai. I was going to go see Arsenal vs. Fulham; that was the truth part. I had emailed a friend of mine in London who I knew had season tickets and we were going to go see the match together. So that was the true part I would end up telling everyone I was meeting with. The part that wasn't true was that I had this "crazy layover" in Dubai to get a lower airfare to London. Regardless, INSEAD Dubai was excited for me to see Arsenal.

As we finished our pancakes we got back on the subject of the American Associate class. INSEAD Dubai said, "If the success rate is so low, maybe they are not hiring the right people."

"I get what you're saying, but all three of the New York hires that were in our class were from good schools. They got their MBAs at Dartmouth, NYU, and UVA. These are top MBA programs. So, it's not a lack of intelligence. If you look at who succeeded in our class, everyone's first account was from a family friend or someone they knew before being a broker. Maybe the only question in the interview should be will your dad help you get new assets for the firm."

"That's sad. Maybe they should hire people's dads."

"The dads won't take the job, so they hire the next best thing."

When it came to American Private Banker's the question of who your family knows always comes up. It even came up for Bud Fox and Jake Moore. It's tough to get those first few clients without family connections.

After breakfast, INSEAD Dubai and I went up to the Credit Suisse offices in The Gate. These offices were about a million times more impressive than 3414 Peachtree Street. The offices took up three floors: 9, 10, and 11. They were sleek and modern and had great views of Dubai. Teams all sat in the same room together. But instead of there being a team crammed into one small office like there is in Atlanta, there was one massive team that would cover all of India and they all sat together in a big room. There was one massive team that covered all of the GCC and they sat together in a big room. It was like what the Atlanta office would be if all of us sat together and covered the entire southeastern United States. Instead of six teams of four or so competing against each other, one team of twenty four working together to cover the southeast. It would be like Voltron. It's an amazing concept, but since the United States still works like stockbrokers, it will never happen.

While walking around and touring all the floors, I asked INSEAD Dubai how he invested for his clients.

"I use MACS."

Just so you know, MACS is an internal Credit Suisse Separately Managed Account run by an internal team.

He continued, "I still have to go out and meet with clients and prospects so I can't be tied to my desk managing a portfolio, so I use MACS. I like them. There are a few people from the MACS team in our office. I can take them on meetings."

I could offer MACS out to my clients too, but my investment philosophy leaned more toward running discretionary accounts with Alex. What I found interesting is that we could offer the exact same investments. We were both called Private Bankers, our jobs were very similar, we could offer the same investments and services to clients. It is so very close to being the same thing.

The main difference was that all I thought about was how to generate enough revenue off prospective clients so that after it got sliced and diced, I would have enough money to survive. All INSEAD Dubai though about was how to best serve his clients and follow up on leads from his team and referrals. He had to work on clients and referrals given to him and bring in clients to get a bigger bonus. I had to bring in clients to survive. No referrals. No clients given to me. Hunt 'em. Kill 'em. Hope there's enough meat left on them after they get sliced and diced so you can eat.

After the tour of the offices, we took the elevator back down to the parking deck where INSEAD Dubai had parked. As we were walking to his car he turned to a row of cars and said, "Oh yeah. I forgot to tell you about this. We get chauffeured to our meetings."

He pointed to a Mercedes, a BMW and a Lexus.

"We have our choice of cars depending on how we want to appear to the client or prospect. Whenever I go to Abu Dhabi, I always take the chauffer. It's really nice."

I couldn't believe it. I was renting a Toyota Prius and driving my ass to Raleigh, North Carolina, for meetings with prospects and he was getting chauffeured to Abu Dhabi in his choice of luxury vehicle.

From what I could tell, being a Private Banker in Dubai was not a bad gig.

INSEAD Dubai dropped me off at my hotel and gave me some ideas on how to spend the rest of the day. I had about twelve hours until my midnight flight. I took a cab to briefly see Jumira and the Gulf. I ate lunch at the Dubai Mall. It was all very impressive, but I wasn't focused on seeing the sites. I was focused on the next part of my walkabout, meeting with London City.

I spent the majority of my day in Dubai at the airport waiting for my flight and thinking about how vastly different my job felt from INSEAD Dubai's job. We were so close yet so far, literally and figuratively.

If the fee based account was the answer to "churn 'em and burn 'em." Was teamwork, salary and bonus the answer for MBAs taking this job seriously? Without teamwork, salary and bonus, the Private Banking MBA program in the United States was a two-year paid cluster fuck with a third year side of go fuck yourself. Who wants that?

What if Major Major Cooper could lead a team of twenty-eight Private Bankers all working together to cover the southeast? One for all and all for one. Doesn't that sound better than six teams trying to knife each other in the back over who gets to cover what prospect and MBAs sending out resumes after twelve months because their salary is going to run out soon? One of my worst moments as a Private Banker was when I was prospecting a massive private corporation. I cold called the CEO and got him. We began emailing with each other and building a relationship. I put the company on the Global Prospecting List to make sure no one else would call on the company. Then, about seven months after my first conversation with the CEO, Credit Suisse announced that it was going to take the company public. I should have been thrilled, but instead Major Major Cooper gave the prospect to another team in the Atlanta office. He didn't tell me and the other team didn't tell me. Major Major Cooper's assistant had to pull me aside and tell me I just got screwed over and there was nothing I could do about it.

"He does this all the time. Gives IPO referrals to the teams he likes even if you have been covering it," she said.

If being a Private Banking Associate is the hardest job in the world, then Major Major Cooper was making it damn near impossible. Sitting in the Dubai Airport, I couldn't stop thinking about how this would make a great Harvard Business School Case. What works better? The team structure and investing of Dubai, or the team structure and investing of Atlanta. Did Major Major Cooper get his money's worth out of Jeremy Jones? Did Major Major Cooper get his money's worth out of Matlock? I think it would be interesting to find out.

CHAPTER THIRTY-SIX

London

When I arrived in London on Sunday, I hadn't really slept since leaving the United States on Thursday. I didn't sleep on the plane to Dubai. I didn't get much sleep in my hotel in Dubai. And, I didn't sleep at all on my red-eye from Dubai to London. I should have been exhausted, but I wasn't. You know when you can't sleep the night before something you are excited about? I was like that every day since I left Atlanta. I just couldn't sleep. I couldn't stop thinking about my next step and the ultimate final challenge: Zur Oepfulchammer. The jump.

Unlike the difficulty I had confirming my meeting in Dubai, confirming my meeting with London City was easy. However, the schedule did change.

Me: I just want to confirm lunch on the 22nd. It will be fun to tell you about the rest of the Associate class. I'm going to be staying near Hyde Park, but send me a time and address and I'll either taxi or tube it over. And thanks for inviting me. Very very nice of you. I've never had an English style lunch and am looking forward to it.

London City: I left Credit Suisse four weeks ago and things have been a bit hectic suffice to say my wife invited her family over for my daughter's birthday party on Sunday and I didn't put two and two together because my calendar didn't have our appointment. I know you are only over here

for a couple of days but could we find
another meal time to meet up? I could do
Sunday dinner instead. I could take you
somewhere exciting. I am really sorry, I
feel absolutely terrible for messing you
around but I will make it up. Let me know
when you can fit me in and I will move
things around. Hope all is well in the US
and I can't wait to hear all the gossip.

Me: No problem. Sunday dinner or a pint would be great. We
could even do a lunch on Monday if that works. Looking
forward to it. PS–lots of gossip.

London City: Sunday dinner works for me.
Where are you staying and what is your
knowledge of London like?

Me: I did a summer internship in London in 1998, but haven't
been back since. I will love pretty much any pub or place to
eat that you suggest.

London City: Do you like spicy food? I know
this amazing proper restaurant, but it is
about 30 mins from where you are staying.

Me: Sounds good to me. Give me a time and place and I'll
be there.

London City: Let's meet at 7:45 pm at
Aldgate East station. Don't wear too flashy

```
clothes and don't play with you mobile
outside the station. We'll walk down to the
restaurant from there. It is on Umbertson
Street off Commercial Road. Call if any
probs. Looking forward to it.
```

I was disappointed that I would never find out what the "all the trimmings" were, but perhaps this "proper restaurant" would have some trimmings. The change in schedule allowed me to truly meet up with my friend at the Arsenal vs. Fulham match, the excuse for my travel to each respective country.

After landing at Heathrow, I took the express train to Paddington station and walked one block to my hotel, The Ascot Hyde Park. I was curious to see what a $73.66 per night hotel in London looks like. As long as it had a bed and a shower, I would be happy. It's amazing how important the size of the beds and rooms are when we are creating our home. But when you are traveling and on your own it really doesn't matter at all. It's just a place to lay your head for a few hours and a place to store you luggage while you are off on your adventure. My room, which was in a great part of London, was on the third floor of a three story walk-up on Craven Rd. It was miniature. There was just enough room for the bed and me. I needed to squeeze past the bed to get to the bathroom, which had just enough space for a shower, toilet and sink. All of which I could reach out and touch while standing in the bathroom doorway. I turned on the shower and it had hot water. Nothing else mattered.

I put on some clean clothes and tubed it over to Putney Bridge to meet my friend and hit the home team pub before the match. I couldn't tell him that I was writing a book either, so when he asked what I was doing in London I said that I was in town for work. I was getting tired of making up excuses, but couldn't tell him the truth. Even to a friend, just the thought of saying it out loud seemed difficult. Maybe if the book was already written, then I would feel comfortable saying, "I wrote a book." But the thought of saying, "I'm writing a book," made me think I sounded crazy. A lot of people are writing books. A lot less finish writing them.

The Arsenal vs. Fulham match at Craven's Cottage proved to be an excellent distraction. The result was a 2-2 draw with goals by some of the top players in the world: Van Persie, Walcot and Zamora. After the match we went to the away team pub for post match pint. I didn't want to leave the pub. It was filled with Arsenal chants and we were having a great time hanging out, but when my buddy said, "I've got the next round, mate," I had to decline. Looking at my watch I had about 45 minutes to get from Putney Bridge to Aldgate East. I needed to leave to make it on time.

"I can't, man. I wish I could, but I can't be late to this."

It was difficult to convince him that one pint after the match was enough, but I needed to get back to my mission. The soccer match was fun, but finding out how Private Banking works in London was my whole reason for being in town. I left the pub and tubed it over to Aldgate East. I looked down at my clothes. Perfect. Not "too flashy." I pulled out my mobile and texted London City that I was on my way, then put it in my pocket per his instructions. I had a feeling this was one of those hidden gem type restaurants where the food is great, but the location is a bit dodgy.

Just like seeing INSEAD Dubai, seeing London City seemed like no time had past since our days of training in Zurich. But now both of us had a little more of a Private Banker look to us. More weathered due to our time in the trenches. The patina of young MBA students had worn off.

The restaurant we went to was called Lahore and the neighborhood reminded me of the Mission in San Francisco. It was Sunday night and packed with a crowd of Pakistani patrons.

"This is some of the best Pakistani food in London. It doesn't look like much, but the food is amazing. I thought you probably didn't have a lot of restaurants like this in the States. I hope you came prepared to eat."

I thought about the last time I ate. It didn't occur to me until that moment, but that had been on my red-eye flight. I hadn't eaten all day. My only sustenance had been four pints surrounding and during the soccer match. I was starving.

"I'm prepared for anything you order."

London City loved food just as much as me and went to ordering: Lassi, Grilled Lamb Chops, Karahi Bhindi Chicken, Chicken Korma, Karahi Chicken Tikka Masala, Lamb Jalfrezi, Karahi Gosht.

After all the food was ordered and we began our feast, London City told his story. He began with the most important part. The money.

"Starting salary for a Private Banking Associate in London is 60,000 pounds plus bonus."

So, the UK and the US got lower salaries than Switzerland and the UAE. 60,000 pounds at the time of our dinner equaled $90,000. Plus he got a year end bonus. All-in about $120,000.

"We always get salary and bonus. There's no year three 100% commission for us."

London City went on to tell about his job as a Private Banker in London. He was the only London Private Banker in my Associate class, so his experience represented the entire country of England in the Associate class of 2009. My buddy LBS, wasn't a Private Banker. He was in the External Asset Managers group and was in training with us. But, he didn't manage money for rich people.

London City's team at Credit Suisse covered Financial Institutions Managers within the firm and outside of the firm. So, his clients were millionaires at Credit Suisse that managed hedge funds and asset manages outside of the firm that managed mutual funds, hedge funds and private equity funds. His team only worked with Financial Institution Managers. Unlike American Private Bankers, he had a very specific focus and didn't just pick up the phone and cold call anyone with a million dollars to invest. He didn't manage money for his dad's friends or some retired guy's IRA. He only worked for Financial Institutions Managers.

After describing the team he was on he said, "When I first started, I inherited 160 accounts generating about 200,000 pounds in revenue."

"What! You inherited accounts?"

"They weren't the best accounts. A lot of them didn't generate money anymore. So, I would call them and pitch them on how we could start doing business together again."

This was his idea of cold calling.

"A lot of new guys won't pick up the phone and call these accounts, but you would be surprised. They'll do business with you if you call them."

Inheriting accounts. Salary. Bonus. These things were becoming a trend. That's how it was for INSEAD Dubai and that's how it was for London City. 160 accounts. 200,000 pounds in revenue. His first day must have been so different than mine. No accounts. No team. A desk sitting next to no one and an email address. That's all I was given. If I was him I would have been pretty damn happy.

"So, why are you now at Barclays?" I asked.

I suppose it made sense that the most British person I've ever known was now working at a British bank, but if he had salary and bonus and 160 accounts at Credit Suisse, why leave?

"I got a head hunter and thought I would see if I could make more money. Credit Suisse wasn't going to up my title or salary. Barclays gave me more money, a higher guaranteed year-end bonus, and made me a Vice President. What's crazy is that after spending all that money on training, Credit Suisse wouldn't match Barclays. And Barclays had to spend a lot to get me. Barclays has to pay the head hunter the equivalent of 60% of my first year's salary. It's crazy."

"Are you taking all your clients with you?" I asked.

"I'll take a couple of the good ones. My assistant and a trainee took over all of my accounts."

Assistants and trainee's taking over accounts. That was unbelievable to me. If anyone in the US left the firm, all the big guys would fight with the manager to get the accounts left behind because it meant more money directly into their pocket for doing nothing. No account in the Untied States would be given to an assistant because of the payment structure in the United States. The Private Banking job in London was very similar to Dubai, but London City wanted a bigger salary and a bigger year-end bonus so he hopped ship for Barclays. It's amazing how different his perspective was from the United States Private Banking Associate class. We were just trying to pay our bills and hope that when our salary was cut to zero our commission wouldn't get sliced up so much that we would be making considerably less. We thought to ourselves, "I sure hope I don't make less." He thought to himself, "I've been here for two years and want to make more." It was a completely different job. He was a Private Banker. The United States Associates were just a bunch of stockbrokers, securities sales reps.

When I asked how he managed money, he said that he used mostly Credit Suisse separately managed accounts. His style of investing was like Jeremy Jones. He would charge 1.3% fee for an all equity portfolio and 0.7% for an all debt portfolio. It was fairly similar to the fees in the United States. He said that best people in the London Credit Suisse office that got the big year-end bonuses were the one's that did big transactional business. Just like in the United States, if you made an introduction to the Investment Bank and the Investment Bank did an IPO or financing for the company you referred, the Private Banker would get a massive year-end bonus. That was the way to make a lot of money in Private Banking in London. Collect your salary and then get lucky bringing in some transactional business to the Investment Bank to get a big bonus.

I asked if there was such a thing as $11 million dollar signing bonuses like Jeremy Jones.

"No. That's not how it works in London. Since we get a salary and year-end bonus here, if someone gets recruited by another firm then they will negotiate a guaranteed year-end bonus. But, it's not $11 million. After a couple of years once the guaranteed high bonus is over, then the Private Banker will leave for another firm. That's how Private Bankers hop around in London."

Throughout our conversation we continued to gorge ourselves on Pakistani food and didn't necessarily always stay on the topic of finance. We would hop around from movies, to music, to TV. Our conversation changed channels like a television. Sometimes we were on CNBC, but we skipped around a lot. We bonded over our love of *The Wire*. He would describe how his mother, who is very posh, would have to watch it with the subtitles on but stilled loved the show. He gave me recommendations for British comedy. I gave him recommendations for TV drama and I was saddened that we didn't hang out more during training in Zurich. London City was an awesome guy. Out of our entire Associate class, he's one of the few I would actually give my money to, if I wasn't giving it all to Sallie Mae.

After paying the bill, London City asked, "Have you ever had Paan?

It's a Pakistani thing that they have after a meal. It's not drugs. But it's got tobacco in it, I think. You chew on it and spit. It turns your spit red. There are streets in England that ban Paan because it stains the street red and you can't get it out. There are literally entire streets stained red because of this stuff. Want to try it?"

"Sure. Why not?"

London City left me at the restaurant entrance and whispered to the host. The host motioned to someone in the kitchen, then from around the corner came a Pakistani guy holding two small plastic baggies. He handed them to London City and we walked out of the restaurant.

"What the heck was that?" I asked. "That seemed like a drug deal out of *The Wire*. Did you see how the one guy just appeared from around the corner?   What is this stuff?"

"That did seem like *The Wire*. Especially these little plastic baggies. It's fine. Just chew and spit."

There we were. Two Private Bankers walking around the dodgy part of London spitting tobacco all over the sidewalk. Two years earlier I never would have thought I would see London City again, but we were having a damn good time. He told me how to take the tube back to Paddington station and we said we would stay in touch on LinkedIn. He said to let him know what happened to the Americans when salary ran out in January and that was it. Part two of the mission was complete.

I went to bed exhausted. It was early Monday morning, the lack of sleep had caught up with me. As I fell into bed my final thought was that I'd forgotten to ask about stockbrokers. If Private Bankers in London get salary and commission forever, then what was all that stockbroker stuff I saw when I did my Factiva search? Seconds later I was asleep.

CHAPTER THIRTY-SEVEN

LBS

I didn't wake up until 2:30pm on Tuesday. That afternoon, I called LBS and scheduled a dinner for 6 p.m. Since LBS wasn't a Private Banker, I didn't consider him to be part of the mission, but I need to thank him for referring the $75 million client to me. And, seeing him was more like hanging out with an old friend because we had kept in touch since our days in training. Maybe he could help me get to the bottom of the question of whether stockbrokers existed in London.

After getting some coffee at the corner Nero's, I showered and put on the only nice pants and collared shirt I packed. LBS and I were going to fancy it up a little and go to OXO Tower for dinner. It was part celebration for his help in landing the big client and part splurge.

I took the elevator up to the restaurant and realized why LBS had picked it. It had the best view of any restaurant in London. I looked around for him and then found him sitting on a barstool—just like in training. We were both fans of going out and spending our per diem at some of the best restaurants and bars in Zurich and it looked like we were starting off on the same foot in London.

He got up from the bar and bear hugged me.

"W.E.! So glad to see you, mate."

"Good to see you too! I can't believe I'm here. Great restaurant pick by the way."

"It's one of my favorites. And, London City said he took you to Lahore yesterday so I thought we would do something nice."

We sat at a table next to a glass wall overlooking the river Thames and got the most important thing out of the way. Ordering. We both love food and even though we had a million things to catch up on we both went straight into the menu: Scottish Langoustines, Suckling Pig, Black Pudding, Honey Cake, Chocolate Soufflé, were just a few things that I recall. Next, I thanked him for the $75 million referral and gave him an update on the steps I had to take to set it up.

"I'm glad you could do it. I was sure that prospect was going to be dead in the water. I wasn't 100% certain they were a legitimate referral," he said.

"I wasn't sure either until I met with them in New York. That's when I realized that it was a huge opportunity. Crazy how things work out."

Our conversation would bounce around from food to family to finance. I was just biding my time and looking for the right moment to ask him about stockbrokers. It was around dessert when we had the first lull in the conversation and I asked, "Do you have stockbrokers in London? You know like Bud Fox from Wall Street. Do you know Bud Fox?"

"Of course I know Bud Fox. Yeah, London still has stockbrokers. Why?"

"Well, I was wondering if the London stockbroker gets paid like the US Private Banker. 100% commission. Eat what you kill."

"London stockbrokers get a salary but it tends to be very low compared to bonuses. Many brokerage houses still operate the system of a low salary plus bonuses twice a year although this practice is changing and moving more toward the salary and discretionary bonus model operated by major banks."

"So, not even stockbrokers that just buy and sell securities are paid 100% commission?" I asked.

"100% commission is a rare model and I think that only the US really still embrace it. The UK transitioned out of that a long time ago. You worried about year three? You just got a massive account. You're golden right?"

"Not exactly. In six months I turn into a stockbroker making $26,000 per year," I replied.

"$26,000? How's that possible? That's 10,000 pounds. That's impossible."

We left OXO Tower and black cabbed it over to the East End so LBS could take me to some bars I would never find on my own. We went to Lounge Lover and the Hoxton. Over bourbon drinks, beers and cigarettes, I explained how landing a $75 million dollar account only equaled $26,000 in salary for me in 2012.

"The thing is," I said, "I feel like if I performed at the same level in any other country outside of the United States, I would be a good banker. But, in the United States I'm a stockbroker making $26,000. It sucks."

"Does every bank in the US pay that way?"

"The only one that doesn't is JP Morgan. They do it like the rest of the world. Salary and Bonus. No one leaves JP Morgan."

"Yeah. They've got a good reputation here, too.

It felt good to kvetch to LBS. We both determined that we had no objection to the "eat what you kill" model of remuneration as long as people are paid a salary that allows them to live a decent life and as long as it doesn't incentivize malpractice. I didn't feel bad about complaining to him a little because we are close friends and I didn't have anyone in the US to complain to. The rules were all the same for us in the states and there was no use complaining. But, it felt good talking to someone who knew the 100% commission model was still only embraced by the US.

"Would you still have taken the job at Credit Suisse if you knew then what you know now?" he asked me.

"Well, $250,000 over two years during the great recession isn't that bad. But if I had to make the choice again, I would do something different. All I thought about was the money and that I knew I was smart and I had a good chance. Eighteen months in to my twenty-four month window and I have to tell you, I don't think I would do it again. MBAs like the idea of Private Banking, but the reality is that in the United States it's just a two year job and nothing more. Everyone starts sending out resumes after twelve months."

After beers at Hoxton, LBS pointed me in the direction of the tube. It was late. He had to work in the morning and I had to finish my mission. Last stop was where it all began: Zurich.

CHAPTER THIRTY-EIGHT

Zurich

I was standing on Banhofstrasse, the exact same place that the book *The Numbered Account* begins. My journey had now come full circle. Maybe it began when I was a freshman in college and my grandmother bought me that book. Maybe it began at that first Associate class dinner in Zurich two years ago. Regardless of where it began, I was back in Zurich on Banhofstrasse at the Renwegg tram stop waiting for Russian Girl.

I arrived in Zurich the night before and checked into my room at the Zic-Zac Rock Hotel. It was a far cry from the $500 a night hotel I stayed at during my month of training, but it was in a good location: only half a block from Zur Oepfulchammer. I could walk to the restaurant from the hotel in about twenty seconds. The only way to describe the Zic-Zac Rock hotel is "funky." It's a rock and roll hotel in the heart of the old city. But it is clean and it is cheap. All the rooms are named after famous Rock and Roll stars or groups. I felt a good omen when I checked into my room. I was next to Supertramp. Maybe McCandless was watching over me.

The night before I had sat on some stone steps next to the river, chain smoking and thinking about my trip so far. Knowing it was almost over. Almost time to make the jump at Zur Oepfulchammer. Now, standing on Banhofstrasse, I was nervous. First off, I was standing where the murder took place in the opening scene of *The Numbered Account*. Second, I had been using my corporate Blackberry to text and email with everyone on my trip. The firm could see all of my communications. What if they figured it out? What if they knew I was writing a book about being a Credit Suisse Private Banker and interviewing employees? Considering that they are known for their Swiss Banking secrecy, they would probably want to stop me. All they had to do was read my emails with Russian Girl to know when and where I was: outside of the Coop at the Renwegg tram station at 11:30 a.m. The meeting place was about a block from Credit Suisse headquarters at Paradeplatz 8. They could just walk over and nab me if they wanted.

It was lunch hour and I was in the middle of a throng of people wearing suits and dark sunglasses. Every time someone in a suit and sunglasses came near me I thought he was going to throw me in the back of a car and take me away.

Russian Girl was late. Maybe she was a spy. I thought about crossing over to the other side of the street so I could see her approach and have a better vantage point. See if she was with anyone. I would be a less easy target that way. The longer I waited, the more details I remembered about the opening scene in *The Numbered Account*. There was a man murdered on Bahnhofstrasse. He had just left Cartier on Bahnhofstrasse and walked over to the tram stop. His throat was slit while getting onto the tram. I looked to my left and there it was: the Cartier on Bahnhofstrasse. This is no joke. I was standing exactly where the Private Banker gets murdered in the opening scene of that book.

I started freaking out. What if that book was some sort of omen? A sign that I ignored. What if something bad was about to happen to me? Maybe it was my fate? I really didn't like this coincidence. When Russian Girl did finally show up, I calmed down. I'm no Jason Bourne, but I could tell she wasn't a spy or a murderer. In fact, it seemed like she was on my side: another Associate Private Banker wanting to talk about their strange experience in the Global MBA training program.

We walked down a side street and sat down at a corner café. The first thing she said after ordering was, "I resigned."

Yeah She was on my side.

"What? What happened?"

Russian Girl suspiciously looked over her shoulder and then whispered, "I process transactions and I don't know where the money comes from. It could say 'for machinery' on it but could actually be used for sex trafficking. I don't know. A woman got taken away by police last year for processing a transaction that was money for a hit. Someone was murdered. The police came to the office and arrested her. She said she had no idea what the transaction was for, but Credit Suisse wouldn't support her. The firm said that it knew nothing about it and blacklisted her. She can't get another job."

"You're joking. This kind of stuff happens?"

"All the time. But it's not just that. When I started I was making 120,000 Swiss Francs per year plus a bonus."

In the back of my mind I thought that just confirmed what INSEAD Dubai told me about the money he got when he started in Geneva.

She continued, "I make a lot of money, but I'm really just a secretary to twenty-five year olds that luckily were given $500 million dollar accounts. None of them have their MBA. They were assistants that just were in the right place at the right time and were given huge accounts to manage. I know more about finance than they do."

Again, here's that theme of accounts being given to people, but Russian Girl wasn't lucky enough to get any given to her. Like INSEAD Dubai's time in Geneva, she was given more of an assistant's role.

"So, you make 120,000 Swiss Francs per year plus bonus. That sounds pretty good. Do you have to cold call or anything?"

"No. Cold calling is illegal in Switzerland. We only network and harvest accounts through existing clients. We are harvesters. The Americans are the hunters."

Amazing. She was making a ton of money and didn't have to cold call. Not a bad job. But there is the whole murder thing.

"You're a Swiss Banker in Switzerland. People dream of this job."

"It's really difficult living and working here if you are not from here. I can't own any property. There's very little chance of me moving up. Plus, I'm so far away from my family. I don't have another job set, but I need to get out of here. This isn't a job for MBAs. Everyone from our class has left Zurich. All Private Bankers are gone. A couple of operations people went to Singapore."

"You're making $142,000 plus bonus. You don't have to cold call. In the United States, we only make $95,000 and then after three years we make $0. Does your salary get cut to zero at the end of your second year?"

"No. That's only an American thing."

I told Russian Girl about the Associate class in the United States. I told her that every New York Associate got fired or quit within the first twelve months. I told her there were only six Associates left out of ten and that most everyone is looking for a new job because salaries will be running out in six months.

In the United States everyone left because they would never be able to support themselves using commissions only. In the UK everyone left because Barclays was paying more money. In Switzerland everyone was getting paid a lot of money, but they were leaving because the job wasn't fulfilling and it was difficult to live in Switzerland if you are not from there. Dubai seemed like the best place to work. No one was leaving Dubai.

Both Russian Girl and I agreed that we hated to see this happen to smart people. We both wanted to be able to warn MBAs that were thinking about interviewing for a job in Private Banking. I especially wanted to warn MBAs in the United States. A Private

Banking Associate job in the US is similar to being an Analyst in Investment Banking because for the vast majority of new hires it is only a two-year program. When 90–100% of new hires leave once salary runs out or before, then how can you think of it any differently?

"So, what are you going to do when your salary runs out?" she asked.

"I don't know," I replied. But I did know that I was going to have to start sending out resumes soon.

We said our good bye's and I told her that I would be in touch in January and let her know what ended up happening to me and the rest of the American Associate class. I walked away from the café and over the river back to the old city thinking to myself, "I love any country where cold calling is illegal. God bless Switzerland. Perhaps the job sucked, but I would gladly take a guaranteed $140,000 plus bonus. I'm not proud. I've got student loans to pay."

CHAPTER THIRTY-NINE

The Short Happy Life of a Private Banker

My life had changed a lot in two years. I flew to Zurich one month after graduation in May 2009 with $0 assets under management and $137,000 in Student Loans. It was now May 2011 and I had $75 million in assets under management and $70,000 in student loans. I was no longer that young, inexperienced MBA. I was a Private Banker with a Swiss client. I was top of my class.

On paper it sounds like I made progress, but in reality I failed and I needed to find a new job. The money and the training in Switzerland and image of Private Banking that seemed so fantastic at graduation turned out to be an unrealistic fantasy. The Private Banking Global MBA Program wasted time and money. It wasted the time of ten MBAs from the United States who would rather have spent the time building a career. And, it wasted the firm's money for paying us and training us in Zurich and New York only for us leave.

The job didn't sound too bad for MBAs working outside of the United States. INSEAD Dubai was making good money. He seemed happy. Hell, he was getting chauffeured to Abu Dhabi! London City left, but it was only because he could make more money elsewhere. He was given accounts to work on and a team to work with. He wasn't going to have his salary cut to 10,000 pounds. He was doing a good job at the bank, but Barclays gave him a raise and made him a Vice President. Russian Girl was making good money. She didn't like the job, but with unemployment so high I don't think there's any shame in taking $140,000 plus bonus and sucking it up. She quit, but I would have taken that money all day long. Everyone was handling their problems with the job differently, but I selfishly thought that my problem was the worst. If everyone else stayed at the firm, they could survive and put a roof over their head and food on the table. I couldn't. And, there were a lot of other Americans out there in the same predicament as me. When your salary is getting cut to $0, you tend to not hear any complaints someone has when they say they make $140,000 plus bonus.

I finally finished all of my interviews and thought that maybe I knew more about the job of Private Banking and Wealth Management than anyone in the world. I certainly was the only one that knew the first time Wealth Management was ever uttered in *The Wall Street Journal*. I knew how Private Banking Associates were paid. I suppose the Private Banking recruiters knew the numbers, but they didn't know what happened to Private bankers on the job and why everyone left the job. Bankers in London probably never knew how guys like Jeremy Jones played the game. And, Jeremy Jones probably doesn't know how guys in London play the game. I knew that the United States was the only country in the world whose stockbrokers were really just Private Bankers. I knew the United States had yet to make the transition like the UK, UAE and Switzerland. I knew that Private Bankers in Dubai had chauffeurs and saw their cars with my own eyes. I knew that the UK actually had stockbrokers and still called them stockbrokers. And, I knew that a little murder every now and then might just be common to Private Bankers in Switzerland.

Every two years, Pricewaterhouse Coopers publishes a report on Private Banking and Wealth Management aptly named "The Global Private Banking and Wealth Management survey." In 2011, PwC surveyed 275 participants from 67 countries, on topics such as clients, human capital, operational performance, market performance and technology. But I have to say if you read their report you will have no idea as to what it feels like to be a Private Banker and how different the job is all over the world even though it has the same title. I felt like I knew the reality behind those numbers that PwC publishes every two years.

I had gotten what I came for. I found out what happened to the rest of the Associate class. I found out what it meant to be a Private Banker outside the United States. I was finally done with Credit Suisse. When I got back to the United States, I would start sending out resumes. I didn't know where life was going to take me, but I was done with Credit Suisse and done with my first job after B-school. MBA students only get one Associate class and I was proud to be a part of the Credit Suisse Private Banking Associate Class of 2009. I was happy I took a week to reconnect with my fellow Associates from around the world and would do my best to keep in touch with them.

Before I flew back to the United States, I wanted to do one last thing. I wanted to do it for me and for all of the Associates that were there with me two years prior when I tried the Zur Opefulchammer jump and failed. This was my way of proving to myself and Switzerland that I'm not afraid of a challenge.

Later in the evening, I laced up my red Nike Zoom Waffle Racer VII's and walked over to Zur Oepfulchammer. I walked up the ancient steps and was greeted by the old man with the white mustache. He knew what I was up to and showed me to a table right under the beam. I ordered a glass of wine and stared at the beam. My adrenaline started pumping. My arms and upper body muscles tightened knowing that they were about to be called upon for an important task. The small room began to fill up. To my left there was a table full of friends meeting for a birthday. Across from me there was a table full of Swiss college kids and by the looks of their gym bags, they were there for the exact same reason as me: the jump. Next to the college kids were an older man and his wife sharing a leisurely dinner. I looked around at everyone and thought to myself that it was time. I had been waiting and preparing for this moment for months. I had completed everything I wanted to complete on my journey. I had sat at on the bench and sipped my wine long enough. It was time to get my butt off the bench and take the beam test.

I stood up and as I laid my hands upon the beam, I closed my eyes and I thought about what happens at the end of a walkabout. I knew that after I jumped all I was going to want to do was to be immediately transported back to my wife. I missed her like crazy.

All week the Talking Heads "This Must Be the Place," from *Wall Street* had been knocking around in the back of my head and I knew that home was where my walkabout was leading me. I knew the jump was a fitting physical challenge to end my journey. I thought about how it symbolized my job. It looked easy at first then turned out to be an amazing challenge. A challenge you can't imagine until you are hanging up there or being hung up on.

I thought about how different the Private Banker's job is in the rest of the world compared to the United States. The Swiss called the US Private Bankers hunters because we truly had to go out and hunt our own clients or we wouldn't make a dime. I thought back on my time at Credit Suisse and knew that when I stepped into the brush, I didn't run. I took my shots. I didn't bag as many lions at

Jeremy Jones or survive as long as Alex Finn, but I took my shots. I wasn't a coward.

As the word coward flitted through my mind, everyone in the room began knocking on the tables, cheering for me to succeed. I was suddenly surrounded by their smiling faces.

I jumped.

If anyone wants to find out if I made it, they will have to go to Zur Oepfulchammer and look for my initials. I'll never tell. To quote Wilson in Hemmingway's *The Short Happy Life of Francis Macomber*, "You're not supposed to talk about it." And, "No pleasure in anything if you mouth it up too much."

I'm not going to be so serious though and end with a Hemmingway quote. I'm a finance guy through and through and obsessed with the movie *Wall Street*. So, I'll leave you with a quote. It's my favorite line from the entire movie spoken by my favorite actor of all-time, Martin Sheen.

"It's yourself you've gotta be proud of, Huckleberry."

EPILOGUE

To Everyone That Watched *Wall Street* and Wanted to be a Stockbroker

There's one last story I would like to tell. One last detail I want to share. I mentioned in my tale a character named Charlie Barry. He was my boss at my first internship I ever had: Bear Stearns from 1997-1998.

One day during my time as a Private Banker at Credit Suisse, I was entering the elevator in the lobby of 3414 Peachtree Street, the incestuous home to many Private Banking firms in Atlanta. As the elevators doors were closing I looked across the elevator bank and saw someone that looked a little like Charlie Barry exiting an elevator. The doors to my elevator closed and reopened again on the 4th Floor. I stepped out and just stood there for a moment. I hadn't seen Charlie Barry in fourteen years. I imagined him owning his own island. The man had everyone in QCOM two years before it went up 2,000%. I had looked for him on the internet and never found anything. Could that have been him? Is that what Charlie Barry would look like in his 50's?

I immediately began mashing the down button. I had to find out.

I walked briskly out of the elevator and looked around. No sign of the man that looked like Charlie. He must have already made it to the parking deck. I began to jog. I didn't want to run. Running is suspicious. A jog is just a guy in a hurry. I entered the parking deck and still didn't see him, so I began to search different levels and found him walking to his car on the lower level.

"Excuse me. Are you Charlie Barry?" I asked.

"Yeah. I'm Charlie Barry." He said with a confused look on his face.

It was him He was fourteen years older and his hair had gone gray, but it was definitely him.

"Charlie! It's W.E. I interned for you back when you were at Bear Stearns. 1998."

He still looked a little confused.

"I sat at a laptop next to your desk. You pitched Qualcomm all day long. You shared an office with a bald Italian guy."

He finally remembered.

"Boy oh boy. You've got a good memory. Those were some crazy times I tell ya. Those Qualcomm days were great. Clients were giving me front row tickets to hockey games. Those were crazy times. What are you doing here? Where do you work?"

We exchanged business cards. Charlie was now working at a small Registered Investment Advisor. Fourteen years later and Charlie and I were working in the same building again. I told him I was at Credit Suisse and he said he would give me a call and take me out to lunch.

The next day my phone rang and on the other end someone said, "W.E., this is your wife's divorce attorney."

It was classic Charlie. He was still using the same line.

"Hey, Charlie. We still on for lunch?"

He sounded disappointed.

"How did you know it was me?"

"Charlie, I spent a year sitting next to you hanging on your every word. I remember all your lines. You were a big influence on me."

That cheered him up and he wasn't so disappointed that I guessed it was him on the line. We set a time to have lunch later that day.

Charlie and I walked across the street to Lenox Mall and ate at the Panera Bread. This is the same mall that I would buy Charlie Chick-fil-A for lunch fourteen years prior. Charlie would never leave his desk back then. He was tied to the stock market.

When we sat down Charlie described how he began his career back in 1982 at Merrill Lynch in New York. Back then he said over half of his office was in their twenties. He said that all you needed back then was a $100,000 account and you could do big business.

"On a $100,000 account we would pump them with shares of IPOs and secondary offerings all day long and make a ton of money. Back then you got paid well on everything."

In the 80's there was no CNBC or internet and getting information to people was a big part of the sale. Some of Charlie's favorite lines he used when cold calling were, "Hey, Mr. Smith, I don't have insider information. I have first hand information! Boy oh boy I tell ya that was a great line." Charlie used to do all of his research and use Merrill's research reports just like Bud Fox and used that to get prospects interested on cold calls. Could you imagine a twenty-something year old kid now pitching Coke stock on the phone to a CEO? It all changed around 1996-1997, the years E-Trade went public and Jeremy Jones joined Goldman Sachs and wealth management was uttered in *The Wall Street Journal* for the first time. For me, those years are the line in the sand.

Charlie's first title was Securities Sales Rep. I stopped him at the mention of his first title.

"Why doesn't anyone use the Securities Sales Rep title anymore?" I asked.

"The Sales Rep title is all about you. No one wants to be sold. Now, everyone is some sort of advisor and it's all about providing advice to help them. Now all the advertising is "What's your number?" Or, "Stay on the Path." Or, "Identify your needs." Now, all anyone talks about is asset allocation and diversification and needs analysis. It's impossible to find anyone in the wealth management business that doesn't use these words. Wealth management is now a commodity. The business started to change from stock pickers to advisors with E.F. Hutton. They changed the business by telling clients that instead of just buying stocks from a broker, they could now buy mutual funds. They could be like Yale or Calpers and choose "managers." That changed everything."

"Do you still pick individual stocks for clients?" I asked.

"No. I was probably one of the last dinosaurs to do that. Position building in a stock is dead. Now I advise clients to diversify using large cap, mid-cap, small cap fund managers. I use foreign fund managers for international exposure. I use bond fund managers for fixed income exposure."

"How has the business changed in terms of how the job is done?"

"Young people have to infiltrate the rich and steal a piece of their portfolio. That's the job of the young guy and when I say young, I mean over thirty. No one does this in their twenties anymore. For older established guys, now they can walk out the door and collect a big bonus because they can guarantee a fee stream every year through their established clientele. You don't have to be a good stock picker anymore."

When Charlie was describing portfolio diversification, he didn't have the passion that he did back when he was recommending companies at Bear Stearns. By taking stock picking away from Charlie, Wall Street took away his sizzle. So, if one of Charlie's clients ever reads this, I hope they pick up the phone and tell him to pick a stock for them. They would be making his day. And, the last time I heard him pick a stock, it went up 2,000%.

After lunch, Charlie and I said our good-bye's and I haven't seen him since. I never saw him in the elevator again and I looked up his firm's website and his name is no longer on the "About Us" page. I may never see Charlie again, but to me he is more Bud Fox than the Bud Fox portrayed in *Wall Street II*. I think that if there are any *Wall Street* fans out there wondering whatever became of guys like Bud Fox you'll see bits of him in brokers like Charlie Barry and Bruce Lee and Alex Finn: guys that began in the business in the 80's and are still in the business. That's where you will find Bud Fox.

AUTHOR BIO

W.E. Kidd is like a lot of recently graduated young professionals. He's just a guy with some student loans and a healthy obsession with his job. He has worked at a lot of firms on the street: Bear Stearns, Merrill Lynch, Wachovia, and Credit Suisse. And, he loves to use pop culture references in his writing. He's basically an indie version of Michael Lewis. Or, a cooler version of Greg Smith.

To learn more about W.E.,

visit www.GeeksWhoCanSchmooze.com.

Made in the USA
Lexington, KY
12 January 2014